KITCHENS, COOKING, AND EATING IN MEDIEVAL ITALY

Historic Kitchens Series

Series Editor
Ken Albala, University of the Pacific, kalbala@pacific.edu

The Historic Kitchens series explores the kitchen scene in specific times and places important in the history of food. Each volume covers the kitchen technology, cooking fuels, vessels and implements as well as who did the cooking in both home and professional kitchens. This is followed by an overview of the ingredients, recipes and modes of service to give a complete picture of the gastronomic moment, with discussion of relevant cookbooks, guides to manners and gastronomic texts to round out the picture.

Books in the Series

The Kitchen, Food, and Cooking in Reformation Germany, by Volker Bach

The Colonial Kitchen: Australia 1788-1901, by Charmaine O'Brien

KITCHENS, COOKING, AND EATING IN MEDIEVAL ITALY

Katherine A. McIver

ROWMAN & LITTLEFIELD
Lanham • Boulder • New York • London

Published by Rowman & Littlefield
A wholly owned subsidiary of The Rowman & Littlefield Publishing Group, Inc.
4501 Forbes Boulevard, Suite 200, Lanham, Maryland 20706
www.rowman.com

Unit A, Whitacre Mews, 26-34 Stannary Street, London SE11 4AB

British Library Cataloguing in Publication Information Available

Library of Congress Cataloging-in-Publication Data
Names: McIver, Katherine A., author.
Title: Kitchens, cooking, and eating in medieval Italy / Katherine A. McIver.
Description: Lanham : Rowman & Littlefield, [2017] | Includes bibliographical
references and index.
Identifiers: LCCN 2017022327 (print) | LCCN 2017023061 (ebook) | ISBN
9781442248953 (Electronic) | ISBN 9781442248946 (cloth : alk. paper)
Subjects: LCSH: Kitchens—Italy—History—To 1500. | Cooking—Italy—
History—To 1500. | Food habits—Italy—History—To 1500. | Cooking,
Medieval—Italy.
Classification: LCC TX653 (ebook) | LCC TX653 .M34 2017 (print) | DDC
394.1/20937—dc23
LC record available at https://lccn.loc.gov/2017022327

Printed in the United States of America

CONTENTS

LIST OF FIGURES

ACKNOWLEDGMENTS

As with my previous book for Rowman & Littlefield, both Ken Albala and Barbara Ketcham Wheaton deserve special recognition. Ken is an inspiration and always so enthusiastic about my work. Once again, he encouraged me to send him a proposal for a new series: The Historic Kitchen, which of course, I did and this book is the result. Barbara's methodology for how to read historical cookbooks provided me with the tools to glean information from medieval recipes and formulate ideas about kitchens, equipment, ingredients, and a number of technical details. This book could not have come alive without Barbara, and her friendship, encouragement, and support are truly appreciated. Spending time in Orvieto in July 2016, I spoke with my good friend Erika Bizzarri about this project and about Sermini's recipe for Grilled Eel, which appears throughout this book. So on an outing with Erika and other friends for lunch at Lake Bolsena, and after consultation with the chef, I was surprised with a serving of grilled eel just as it was prepared in the middle ages—a recipe, apparently, well known at that restaurant. What a treat that was! As well, my editor, Suzanne Staszak-Silva, deserves mention for her patience and understanding as, once again, deadlines slipped by and Karen Ackermann, Assistant Managing Editor, has been extremely helpful with the final edits of the manuscript and coordinating the publication process. Finally, I wish to thank my husband, William C. McIver, and many friends who listened patiently, kept me focused, and offered never-ending support throughout the process.

CHAPTER 1

COOKING IN THE MIDDLE AGES
An Introduction

The modern twenty-first century kitchen has an array of time-saving equipment for preparing a meal: a state-of-the-art stove and refrigerator, a microwave oven, a food processor, a blender, and a variety of topnotch pots, pans, and utensils. We take so much for granted as we prepare the modern meal—not just in terms of equipment, but also the ingredients, without needing to worry about availability or seasonality. We cook with gas or electricity—at the turn of the switch we have instant heat. But it wasn't always so. Just step back a few centuries to say the 1300s and we'd find quite a different kitchen, if there was one at all. We might only have a fireplace in the main living space of a small cottage. If we were lucky enough to have a kitchen, the majority of the cooking would be done over an open hearth; we'd build a fire of wood or coal and move a cauldron over the fire to prepare a stew or soup (see Figure 1.1). A drink might be heated or kept warm in a long-handled saucepan, set on its own trivet over hot cools or beside the fire. Food could be fried in a pan, grilled on a gridiron, or turned on a spit. We might put together a small improvised oven for baking tarts, savory pies, and other pastries. Regulating the heat of the open flame was a demanding task. Cooking on an open hearth was an all-embracing way of life, and most upscale kitchens had more than one fireplace with chimneys for ventilation. One fireplace was kept burning at a low,

Figure 1.1 The Cook in his Kitchen, detail of Luttrell Psalter (1335–1340), MS 42130, fol. 207r. British Library, London, UK. Source: Commons.Wikimedia.org.

steady heat at all times for simmering or boiling water, and the others used for grilling on a spit over glowing, radiant embers. This is quite a different situation than in our modern era—unless we are out camping and cooking over an open fire.

Even with this complex manner of cooking so foreign to us, people in the Middle Ages knew how to eat well. By the fourteenth century, Italians had developed certain habits in the areas of food and cooking—comfortable eating habits from which they derived a great deal of pleasure. As we will see, in the thirteenth and fourteenth centuries, the menus that the professional cook dealt with on a day-to-day basis were well-rounded meals of sippet, which was a solid piece of food such as bread used for dipping in liquid food, stews, meat pies, vegetable torts, flans, biscuits, roasts, sauces, aspics, and sweets.[1] How these dishes were cooked and what equipment was used forms the basis of our exploration of medieval cooking practices and techniques.

This, then, is the story of the medieval kitchen and its operation from the late thirteenth century until the mid-fifteenth century. This timeframe marks the heyday of medieval cookery. The Middle Ages, from the fall of Rome in the fifth century to the beginning of the Renaissance in the mid-fifteenth century, is a vast period that spans one thousand years of history and is impossible to grasp in the little space we have here; even the last two hundred or so years is daunting. In this book, we will explore the medieval kitchen from its location and layout using examples like the two kitchens in the merchant Francesco Datini's townhouse in Prato, to its equipment (the hearth, the fuels, vessels, and implements) and how they were used, to who did the cooking (man or woman) and who helped. We'll look at the variety of ingredients (spices, herbs, meats, fruits, vegetables) and food preservation and production (salted fish, cured meats, cheese making), and we'll look through recipes, cookbooks, gastronomic texts, household inventories, letters, and literary works to complete the picture of cooking in the medieval kitchen.

We begin with a look at the oldest known cookbook from the Italian peninsula, the anonymous *Liber de coquina*, written in Naples during the Angevin rule, and stop with the transitional work of Maestro Martino, *Il libro de arte coquinara* or *The Art of Cooking* (1470s). Written originally in Latin, the *Liber* set the stage for later works such as the anonymous Tuscan's *Libro della cucina* written in Italian during the fourteenth century. His book, like the *Liber*, opens with simple recipes for vegetables. Whereas the anonymous Venetian, in his *Libro per cuovo*, also of the fourteenth century, like other writers discussed vegetables in a later chapter, Maestro Martino started his cookery book with meats.[2] Maestro Martino, master cook to Cardinal Trevisan, Patriarch of Aquilea, wrote the "last of the great medieval cookbooks, but it points the way to the next period" and so this is where our story ends.[3]

Cookery books were the subject of the fourteenth-century writer, Gentile Sermini, who created a character of an epicurean parish priest, one Ser Meoccio d'Aquapendente of Pernina near Siena. This priest disguised his favorite cookbook as a breviary, which he read assiduously, pretending to be immersed in pious contemplation. The breviary was entirely filled with recipes by cooks describing all the dishes and delicacies that could be made, how they should be cooked, with what herbs, and in what season; it was all this and nothing else that filled his mind even when Meoccio preached a sermon. In subsequent chapters, we will return to this cookery book and Meoccio's menu for a gluttonous

San Vincenzo's day celebration.[4] Let's turn now to recipe manuscripts, gastronomic texts, literary works, and personal letters to understand how the cook equipped and staffed his kitchen and planned and executed a meal.

The Cook and the Written Word: Medieval Cookbooks

We begin with our primary source, the medieval cookbook. The earliest extant recipe manuscripts were written towards the end of the 1200s; writing down recipes and collecting them into books was relatively rare until the fifteenth century, and for the most part, reflect aristocratic and upper class tastes. Costly and time consuming to produce because scribes had to handwrite the recipes on expensive vellum, most recipe manuscripts were affordable only for the elite and were likely written with them in mind.[5] After all, the professional medieval cook did not necessarily need to consult a recipe, having learned and fixed in his memory the quantities, processes, final flavorings, and appearances of each dish. However, as we shall see, many of the anonymous texts from the thirteenth and fourteenth centuries seem to address the cook's apprentice or assistant. So when a cook decided to write out his recipes, his intended audience could have been an aspiring assistant or his boss; in the latter case, the book went to the library rather than to the kitchen. It could also serve as a record of the writer's career. During our investigation, we will look at such works as the Angevin cook's *Liber de coquina*, anonymous Venetian's *Libro per cuoco*, the Milanese physician, Maino de Maineri's *Opusculum de Saporum*, a health handbook (1330s), and Johannes Bockenheim's *Il registro di cucina di Papa Martino V* (ca. 1420s).[6] These texts not only provide us with recipes, but also tell us about ingredients (including their health benefits) and food preparation. Through the descriptions of how food should be prepared, we will learn about kitchen technology and the process of cooking, about the pots and pans, the gridirons and spits, and the combinations of ingredients. With the exception of Johannes Bockenheim and Maestro Martino, whose books were written in the fifteenth century, the writers of our medieval cookbooks were unknown cooks. Likely, they were employed by a nobleman, a prelate, or some other elite, as is often noted by the editors of the printed editions of these works, such as that of the *Liber de coquina*. These books are a vital source, allowing us to reconstruct the recipes and to understand the various processes and tools used by the medieval cook to prepare a meal.

Surprisingly, the recipes are written in a variety of ways. Often the author made assumptions about his audience, their experience and knowledge, and sometimes gave us an idea of who ate the dish. In Bockenheim's case, for example, the seventy-four recipes are each dedicated to a specific person or class—noble, religious, courtier, or peasant—suggesting to us that at times the papal court hosted some-one from every level of society.[7] Written in Latin, Bockenheim's recipes are brief, simple, and straightforward, noting ingredients, but without giving the quantities, the number of people to be served, or suggesting how a dish could be embellished or modified for a particular taste. If anyone used this book to cook from, which seems unlikely, that cook would have had to determine just about everything before preparing the dish. In contrast to Bockenheim's recipes, the manner in which the Anvigen cook (*Liber de coquina*) wrote his recipes suggests that they were meant for a real cook, starting with the simplest recipes for cabbage and other vegetables and moving on to more complex dishes. He stated in his introduction: "Since we wish to discuss cooking and different kinds of food in this work, we will start with vegetables as the first group of foods . . . delicate cabbages for the gentry" which is used to accompany meats.[8] Thus what had once been strictly a peasant dish, with some additions and its treatment as a side dish, cabbages and other vegetables become acceptable to the upper classes as our cook explained: "Prepare some delicate cabbages, of the sort to which gentlemen of distinction" or "These fragrant leafy greens may be served to persons of distinction."[9]

The *Liber de coquina*, like Bockenheim's book, was written in Latin, and the recipes reflect the tastes of the elite. Unlike the *Liber*, Bochenheim did not include vegetables as a separate dish nor did he include recipes for ravioli or other pastas. Rather, he started with soups ("minstra") followed by meats and tortas, though there is a rec-ipe for *Piatto di erbe* (a plate of greens) for courtiers and their wives, and his Lenten recipes include a variety of vegetable soups and grains followed by recipes for fish and sauces.[10] More importantly, the *Liber* was particularly influential to the anonymous Tuscan whose cookery book is almost an Italian version of the *Liber*. Following the Angevin model, the Tuscan writer began his book with cabbages, but also expanded the selection of greens and root vegetables with other such as turnips and leeks, thus reflecting local tastes.[11] These recipes on ways to cook vegetables suggest that the cook was adapting to whatever was in the market or in the garden, and this is an unassuming way of cooking characteristic of his recipes for vegetables.[12] Unlike our Tuscan cook, the anonymous Venetian writer took another path, beginning his book with broths, though he does include vegetables in a later chapter. Other books, such as Maino de Maineri's *Opusculum de Saporum*, are meant as health manuals rather than cookbooks. However, chapters 10 to 21 of Maino's book survey everything a person of the time was likely to eat and includes recipes for sauces and condiments—thus it has been referred to in modern literature as "the Medieval Sauce Book."[13]

In writing his recipes, the cook often tells us exactly what is needed in the kitchen, perhaps not directly, but through his listing of ingredients as they are used in the recipe and through his explanation of how to make the dish. We also learn how the kitchen functioned and who was needed to pull it all together, whether it was an elaborate dish like *Torta Parmigiana* or a classic like *Blancmange*, a white dish made of white chicken meat, rice sugar, and sometimes almond milk.[14] In this role as recipe writer, the cook becomes, first and foremost, a teacher passing on his knowledge and his ideas; in some ways, the recipe manuscripts are also a record of his career. As well, the cook tells us what was commonly eaten and what might be a special dish—one not found in every recipe book, such as the Venetian writer's recipe for *Torta Manfredi*, honoring the king.[15] The anonymous Tuscan and others often have suggestions for more than one way to make a dish or how it can be served as we see in the anonymous Tuscan's recipes for gourd ("zucche," not squash as we would think today, which is a new world vegetable): the first recipe is simple with the gourd being cooked with pork, whereas in the second one, the ingredients (gourd, spices, and cheese) are all smashed together to become either ravioli stuffing or part of a pasticcio.[16] And the cook gives advice: "save the water from boiling peas," "season as you wish," "better to eat hot," "boil in plenty of water," or "color as you wish." He also includes warnings: concerning eel pie, "let it cool a bit or rich people will burn their mouths" or "make the dough thin enough or it will not please the rich."[17]

Just one recipe can tell us so much about cooking practices, equipment, ingredients, the kitchen staff, and more. Take for example the anonymous Tuscan's recipe for one of the richest creations of medieval cookery the *Torta Parmigiana*, one of the most complex variations of this torta. We will compare it to anonymous Venetian's simpler version.[18] Invented in the Middle Ages, the torta, or pie, was comprised of a crust, top and bottom, and could be filled with any number of ingredients from a simple mixture of eggs, cheese, milk, spices, herbs, and greens, to a complex layering of ravioli, sausages, chicken, pork, spices, and more. It was extremely practical, easy to keep and to eat, and was common to all levels of society. While we will certainly look at other recipes as we explore the workings of the medieval kitchen, this labor-intensive *Torta Parmigiana* will be particularly useful for learning about equipping and staffing the kitchen, food preparation, cooking methods, and ingredients (see chapters 2, 3, and 4).

The Tuscan writer begins his recipe by instructing us on how to prepare the chicken, including chopping onions to fry with the chicken; while the chicken is cooking, we pulverize various herbs "fortemente" with a knife and mix them with grated aged and fresh cheese for the white ravioli (see Appendix I). Parsley and other aromatic herbs are mixed with fresh cheese and egg for green ravioli. Almonds are crushed and mixed with spices, sugar, and eggs for sweet ravioli. But what about the dough to enclose that filling? Not a word about that nor anything about how to cook them. Pork sausage is made; prosciutto crudo is chopped. Eggs, chicken, and salt are mixed until fine. Top-quality flour is used for the crust and made into a round form like a "padella" (pan), and so on. Once everything for the torta is ready, the layering begins: chicken broth is spooned into the shell, then some meat and chicken, next white ravioli, then prosciutto and sausage, another layer of meat, another of sausage, then the sweet ravioli with dates, finally meat broth and spices; the top crust is rubbed with lard and it is ready to bake. But what happened to the green ravioli and how do we bake it? Do we bake it in an oven, or is the baking dish with the torta placed between two red hot slabs of stone or earthenware pushed into the embers of a hearth? How many people will this recipe feed? What about the quantities of ingredients? He only states periodically "in bona quantita" (in good quantity).

The Venetian writer's torta (see Appendix II) will serve twenty-five people, and he specifies the quantities of ingredients and how to bake the torta (over a low flame). There are twelve green ravioli and nine white, and they are boiled before placing them in the torta; there are no sausages or prosciutto, yet he specifies the exact herbs and spices to use. However, he does not specify how to put it all together—everything seems to be dumped into the shell. From both recipes, we learn several processes: dismembering, cutting up and frying chicken, boiling meats, pounding and pulverizing herbs and meat, chopping onions, grating cheese, and more. To do all this, we need knives, spoons, mortar and pestles, graters, pots and pans, and all manner of equipment, but all that is for subsequent chapters.

But what did the Tuscan writer assume by omitting certain processes like making a broth, making the pasta for the ravioli stuffing, baking the torta, and so on? Would another cook turn to other recipes in the book for answers or was he well-versed enough to know exactly what to do? This one recipe has so much to tell us, yet we will have to turn to other recipes to find out about roasting or making sauces or cooking vegetables and fish.

With just these two recipes, we can learn so much about the workings of the medieval kitchen. Just think how many people it would take to make the Tuscan's torta with all the parts that go into it. First of all, the master cook would have significant planning to do to pull it off, making sure he had all the ingredients at hand and ready for prepping—there might be some shopping to do—organizing his kitchen brigade, and setting them to work. And how well equipped was his kitchen? And how many tortas would he need to make to serve twenty-five guests? How long would it take to make all the parts (everything would have to be ready before assembling) and how long would it take to bake? We will find answers to these questions in the following chapters.

The Cook's Voice

The cook's voice, as he narrates his recipes, is the thread that runs throughout this book. We hear him "speaking" as we read through the recipes—almost as if we are voyeurs peering through a door into the kitchen or over the cook's shoulder as he writes. The cook reveals to us both his inventiveness and his practical nature as he chooses from an array of recipes memorized as an apprentice, suggests variations and embellishments, and gives advice. We learn if he is writing for someone with knowledge of cooking or a collector of books or his master. Some cooks, like the Venetian, seem to "talk" to his apprentice or assistant who may one day replace him as head cook. From the outset it is clear that the Venetian writes for the cook as the title of his book implies: *Libro per cuoco* (*The Cook's Book*).[19] He narrates his recipes in a very personal, almost intimate voice using the familiar form of you—"tu" rather than the formal, "vuoi"—for example, the first line of his *Torta de herbe* (Tart of greens) reads "Se tu voy fare torta de herbe per 12 prelate" (If you want to make herb pie for twelve people)."[20] Most of his recipes start out with this phrasing or he begins his recipe with the familiar rather than formal verb tense—for his *Torta ungaresca per 12 persone*, he writes "Toy un capone ben grasso e toy uno lombolo de porco grande" (Take a well-fattened capon and take a large piece of pork), which suggests that he was thinking of either an equal, another cook or an assistant—we almost picture him in the kitchen telling them what to do.

Other cooks' voices are formal and distant. Take Johannes Bockenheim, for example, writing for Pope Martin V and his court, his recipes are only brief formulas (originally in Latin, but later translated into Italian) and he always uses the same formula: "Cosi si fa la minstra di pane, Prendi" (If you want to made bread soup, Take) or "Cosi si preparano le costolette" (If you want to prepare cutlets). Most writers' voices fall somewhere in between the two, neither formal nor intimate, like the Tuscan writer who starts right out with the method: "Togli fave bene infrante" (Take well-crushed fave) or "Togli Polli" (Take chickens), although he does sometimes say: "Se voy fare" (If you want to make). Whereas the Angevin cook (*Liber de coquina*) begins each recipe with "Per fare" (In order to make), "Per fare pasticcio" (In order to make a pasticcio), "per cucinare cavoli" (in order to cook cabbage), and so on (the original was Latin; however, I am using the Italian edition so that the comparison with other writers' voices is clear). Not only do the voices of our cooks vary, but so too their approach to writing recipes, whether it is a simple dish of cabbage or a complex torta. How much detail is there? Do we know how many people the dish will serve or how many eggs we might need? Does the cook assume we will know how much of each ingredient we will need, or does he explain it all as if teaching us to cook? We've already seen how varied our two recipes for *Torta Parmigiana* are, yet both of them are informative. The Tuscan recipe is flexible, allowing the cook to decide, once he knows the number of people to serve, just how much of each ingredient is needed to make each part. He is addressing an experienced cook who knew how to make ravioli, sausage, broth, and so on; whereas the Venetian version is instructive, telling us just how many people his recipe will serve and the exact amount of each ingredient we will need to pull it off. But we will look more closely at these and other recipes in later chapters.

In summary, we can say that early recipes plunge right into the action with opening instructions like "take" followed by a string of ingredients. The earliest cooks prepared and chopped everything before cooking.[21] Cooks typically led a team of trained subordinates, so their instructions assumed that many steps, such as boning and chopping of fish and simmering of rice for blancmange, would be performed in parallel rather than in sequence and used terms, such as pound, without explanation. Recipe instructions suggest the equipment available to the cook. The cook designed meals around the larder or garden. This is reflected in such statements as calling for "sweet spices" or "greenery for color." If a pig had just been killed, a cook would substitute pork for the veal or the chicken specified in the recipe. In winter, dried herbs replaced fresh. As we follow our cook through his kitchen in subsequent chapters, listening to him as author, we learn about the medieval kitchen, the staff, how the kitchen was equipped, ingredients, food preparation, and who ate the dish. Literary works, such as poems and short stories, as we will see in another section, supplement this knowledge. But first let's consider literacy.

Women Who Cook, Literacy, and Recipes

How literate was the recipe writer? Did he dictate his recipes to a scribe, or was he able to write the recipes himself? This remains unclear, but is of some significance for us if we are to understand who the author was addressing and why he wanted to record them at all. We can address this question to a certain degree by looking at Margherita Datini (1360–1423), who recorded recipes and her thoughts about food in her letters to her husband, starting with a brief biographical sketch. Coming from a disgraced noble family, she would have had at least elementary skills in writing and reading when she married Francesco Datini (ca. 1335–1410) in Avignon in 1376. Her father, Domenico Bandini, was decapitated for his involvement in the plot to overthrow the Florentine government, though at one time the Bandini were members of the governing class, holding high office regularly. On the maternal side, the Gherardini were of minor Florentine nobility well above Francesco's station. Once widowed, her mother Dainora moved the family to Avignon where Margherita became the bride of the wealthy merchant from Prato, Francesco di Marco Datini, the first son of a tavern keeper, bringing a small dowry of four hundred florins, thus reflecting the Bandini's view of Francesco's lower social status.[22] Once they were back in Prato (1383) and as time progressed, Margherita managed the house and its staff and conducted business for her husband when he was away from Prato, which was often, and by the late 1380s and 1390s she was perfecting her writing and reading skills. She knew how to cook and had recipes—perhaps only in her memory as part of a verbal tradition. Her letters (the majority of them were dictated to a scribe) to Francesco included recipes; she instructs him on how to cook peas, for example. They were dried peas that she cooked as if fresh, boiled with onions and herbs.[23] And she knew how to cook mushrooms, which she sent to Francesco when he was in Florence, and veal, too. Margherita could make verjuice and pork gelatin. Where did she learn these skills? Would she have had a cookbook, though there are none listed in the Datini household inventories? Moreover, it would have been unusual for a woman raised in a noble household to cook, yet she did once married. Perhaps she observed a cook in her mother's household or in her own. After all, she did have servants to assist her. Francesco, too, knew about cooking; for example, he wrote to Margherita telling her to make the pork gelatin as he had done. As the son of a tavern keeper, he may have had first-hand experience. As well, Francesco, of course, had far superior reading and writing skills than his wife. What about the professional cook? Would he have been, like Margherita, semi-literate? It is of interest to speculate, given the number of medieval cookery books.

And it is an issue to keep in mind as we move into the kitchen with the professional cook and sort through a number of recipes to consider equipment, technique, and ingredients.

The Literary Sources: Poems, Short Stories, Household Inventories, and Personal Letters

Cookbooks are not our only source of information about the kitchen, cooking, and food. Medieval literature is rich with vivid tales of eating, cooking, and acquiring ingredients. Poems, short stories, household inventories, and personal letters add to our knowledge of equipping and staffing the kitchen, a favorite or common dish, and even cooking methods. As well, we learn about what was available in the market in Antonio Pucci's poem about the old market in Florence, how to eat macaroni in Franco Sacchetti's poems, and feasting in the sonnets of Simone Prudenzani and the short stories of Gentile Sermini and Giovanni Sercambi.[24] We have already met one parish priest who was passionate about food, Sermini's priest, Ser Meoccio, with his cookery book hidden in his breviary. We begin this exploration with the Datini inventories and letters, a unique and well-preserved set of documents for this period.[25]

The wealthy merchant Francesco Datini bought up property surrounding the small house he inherited from his father in order to build the Palazzo Datini, one of the largest and most expensive houses in Prato at this time, valued at one thousand florins. It included a large and well-appointed kitchen on the ground floor and a smaller one on the upper floor under the roof.[26] Household inventories taken over a period of years tell us about those kitchens, how they were equipped, what varied tasks were undertaken there, and much about the family itself. It is through the letters between him and his wife, Margherita, that we learn so much about what foods were grown or bought, about their own kitchen gardens, a special or favorite dish, a little about who did the cooking, and also a few recipes. Francesco and Margherita liked food and eating and wrote about it often; for example, he penned a detailed order for dinner: "A good broth (preferably from chicken and capons) with full fat cheese of one kind or another to eat with the broth

. . . some fresh eggs, several fine fish from the Bisenzio river near where they lived, and if there are some (fish) in the market that are still alive and are fresh and good, take several pounds and many good figs and also peaches and walnuts and look to it that the table be well laid and the room well cleaned."[27] And who did the cooking and what were they going to do with the fish and fruit? Most often Margherita cooked for her husband or supervised one of her servants to do it; however, if it was a special occasion such as the wedding of his daughter, Ginevra, then Francesco hired a professional cook.[28]

When he was in Florence, Margherita (in Prato) sent him eggs, fowl, game, cheese, vegetables, and fruit, while he in turn sent home spices, comfits, salted fish, and other delicacies.[29] From his letters, we learn that Francesco sent food as gifts—partridges, for example—and that his own vineyard yielded Trebbiano, Vernaccia, and Greco wines, some of which he kept, some he sold. The Datini garden produced a range of herbs, garlic, onions, chickpeas, and fava beans, which Ser Lapo Mazzei, Francesco's notary, described as, "so tender they melt before you get them in the pot."[30] From both his letters and account books, we learn that Francesco's cheese came from Parma, his eels from the lagoons of Comecchio, and his bread, a good country loaf made with flour from his own wheat, was baked at home, in their baker's oven in their garden across the street from the palazzo in Prato.[31] He enjoyed ravioli made from wheat meal paste and stuffed with pounded pork, eggs, cheese, a little sugar, and parsley, then deep fried in lard, and rice cooked in almond milk with lots of sugar and honey.[32] His account books inform us that the veal he loved was costly at nine florins a piece and that he ate great quantities of fish.[33] We can use this information from their letters and household inventories in much the same way we use the recipe manuscript books—they will fill in the missing parts of our story in the following chapters; but for now, we turn to the poems and short stories.

Some poems, like Antonio Pucci's (1310–1388, a Florentine poet) about the Mercato Vecchio in the heart of Florence during the time of the early Medici family, tell us about what foods were available and in demand—you could buy chicken, hare, boar, and pheasants as well as cheese and herbs; moreover, there were ravioli and torte, figs and peaches and on the list goes.[34] Some poems, like those of Lorenzo il Magnifico de Medici (d. 1492, defacto ruler of Florence), are actual recipes; he had an expert cook, Giovanni, who was a master at making a sweet called *Cialdoni*: "take a glass of water and flour in the best quantities and mix together as if making maccheroni."[35] Other poems, like those of Simone Prudenzani (active in Orvieto 1387–1446) are a conversation. His sonnets called *Il Saporetto* are about the past, imaginary court of Pierboldo, Signore of Buongoverno; there is dance and music, games and hunts, a Lenten meal and wine, we have full menus and descriptions of dishes such as *Tortelli in Scudella* (#59), and a dinner with il signore and his guests: the meal begins with ravioli and lasagna in broth, and with soups in the French style; boiled meats and rich game stews come next, then roast game birds, followed by torte and other savory meat pies. Dried fruit and spices conclude the meal.[36] Yet perhaps the richest sources with the widest range of material are the short stories of Giovanni Sercambi from Lucca, who describes an informal supper in the countryside consisting of salad, lasagna, and an omelet, or his tale of Dante's dining experience at the court of Naples. Or the Sienese writer, Gentile Sermini, whose gourmet parish priest hid a cookery book in his breviary whom we have already encountered; many of his other stories are about food, cooking, and eating. Or Franco Sacchetti, who not only describes a kitchen, but also tells a tale of two peasants sharing a platter of steaming hot macaroni: Noddo d'Andrea, using his fork, wolfs it down while his friend remained hungry with his first mouthful still on his fork.[37] From these poems and short stories we learn about ingredients, a favorite meal, how to eat, prepping and cooking a meal, kitchens and their equipment, and recipes like Gentile Sermini's *San Vincenzo's Day Roasted Eel.*

In the following chapters, we will follow the cook in the kitchen as he prepares for the day. We will learn about its layout and equipment and about his staff and what they must do each day. What is he thinking? What is he planning? Each day the cook must survey his kitchen, making sure everything is in place and in working order. The recipes he learned from memory as an apprentice, he now records—sometimes he is very specific, yet at other times he assumes the reader has the experience and knowledge to interpret them. His recipes and the literary sources we've discussed above are vital tools in our journey to discover the workings of the medieval kitchen. To add a "human" touch to this ideal world of the medieval cook, we will follow, as well, Margherita and Francesco Datini, walking through their kitchens, surveying their equipment and ingredients, understanding their household and how it functioned in comparison to the professional one. They will show us about preparing verjuice, a reduced, tangy liquid made from the early juice of a particularly tart variety of grape and pork jelly, and we will read in her letters Margherita's recipes and her instructions to Francesco about cooking. They are, in a way, our window into the "real" world of the medieval kitchen; their household inventories and personal letters are critical to our story.

CHAPTER 2

THE COOK AND HIS STAFF

In this chapter, we turn to see who did the actual cooking, whether it is in a noble townhouse or a humble cottage. In a peasant cottage or lower-class household, it was usually a woman—wife, sister, or mother—if any real cooking was done at all; often food was purchased on the street, at a tavern, or at a bakery. The kitchens of any large household were staffed entirely by men, from the head cook to the scullery boy, and the same applied to caterers whose services could be called on for wedding parties and other special occasions, whereas in small households, the cook might well be a woman, the housewife, herself.[1] In Francesco Datini's home in Prato, for example, either his wife, Margherita, or other women of the household did the cooking. Yet, when it came to his daughter's wedding in 1407, Francesco hired a cook, Mato di Stincone, "cuoco" and paid him four florins, ten scudi for the single meal (a maid earned ten florins a year) and he hired six other servants besides his own to wait at tables—they were given new tunics of scarlet cloth and hose.[2] A grand and noble household with its own kitchen staff was designed to be self-sufficient, able to provide all the cooked staples and luxuries the master required. Borso d'Este, duke of Ferrara in the 1450s, for instance, had cooks to prepare meals for his staff and guests; his own personal cook, Maestro Zohane, who prepared all his meals even when the duke was traveling; and he had a master confectioner who prepared a variety of sweets for the duke and his guests.[3] Manuscripts, like the *Ordine e officij de casa* written for the

Duke of Urbino, give us a sense of what was required of the kitchen staff in an upper-class household; it specifies the number of cooks, their helpers, and their duties; the head cook, for example, oversaw all that went on in the kitchen, delegated tasks to other cooks, consulted with the steward in planning menus, and in general made sure that his kitchen ran smoothly and that it was clean.[4] From recipes like the one for *Torta Parmigiana* (see Appendix I and II), we can infer just what staff was needed to prepare this complicated dish as we will do later in this chapter.

Hierarchy in the Kitchen

In the Middle Ages, the head cook in a noble household was not the ultimate authority in matters of food, and what went on in his kitchen was by no means determined by him alone. The kitchen was merely one element in the household's operation, and the cook was just another employee with specialized knowledge, abilities, and above all, responsibilities.[5] Rather it was the *maestro della casa* (housemaster) who oversaw the many activities in the palace, including all the people who prepared food and drink, and he hired the cook. Interestingly, at Borso d'Este's court in Ferrara (ca. 1450s and 1460s), his *sescalco* (head steward) served both as a housemaster and head steward. Gatamelata, as he was called, took orders directly from Borso.[6] The environment in the medieval kitchen was rigid and each staff member had his place: the kitchen steward came first followed by the master cook, the undercook, the roasting cook, the person cooking soups and vegetables, the person in charge of the larder and cold foods, the sauce cook and the fruiter, and finally, the scullery boys.[7] This hierarchy was meant to maintain order, to limit waste, and to prevent theft or at least limit how much was taken away by any one of the kitchen staff. The kitchen steward was responsible for maintaining order and for all the expenses, for the daily acquisition of foodstuff, and for the periodic granting of contracts for kitchen supplies. Anywhere from one to three cooks could be in charge of the kitchen work of preparing the food; the master cook regulated what went on and was obeyed in the kitchen.[8] So we turn now to the cook, his duties and responsibilities, and will return to the staff later in this chapter.

The Cook

Platina wrote of the head cook:

> One should have a trained cook with skill and long experience, patient in his work and wanting above all to be praised for it. He should be absolutely clean of any filth or dirt and rightly know the strength and nature of meats, fish and vegetables so that he may understand what ought to be roasted, boiled or fried. He should be alert enough to discern by taste what is too salty or too flat. . . . He should not be gluttonous or greedy . . . so as not to appropriate and devour food intended for his master.[9]

The cook, himself, had to know his position in the hierarchy of the household, had to acknowledge his formal responsibilities to his superiors, had to organize and accept responsibility for those who worked under his authority, and had to ensure that supplies of foodstuffs, fuel, utensils, and labor never failed when they were needed. Most cooks possessed a broad professional repertoire of dishes suitable for various occasions—and he had to be skillful in executing the most appropriate preparations to fulfill those functions. The cook had to make sure he never did anything to impair or endanger the health of his employer, his family, or his guests. The medieval cook was a craftsman, sometimes an artist who both excited and then satisfied the taste of his employer.[10] A master cook often sat between one of the fireplaces and the sideboard on a high chair in order to survey the entire room. The large wooden ladle he held, generally used to sample food, was also used to keep the kitchen staff in line.[11] The cook began his day before dawn by lighting the fire, or stoking a low overnight fire, placing water on to boil, and cleaning vegetables and poultry (see Figure 1.1).[12] He had to check the amounts and quality of supplies and assign various chores. As the hour of the first meal approached, work became increasingly frenetic and the authority of the head cook was essential. He had to know how to take charge and command the respect of his team of an undercook, helpers, and apprentices.

A gifted cook should have the power to bewitch the palate and transform ingredients. Experienced cooks knew that recipes were not cut in stone, but written to be played with and patted into shape as circumstances demanded or tastes decreed. No dish was irreplaceable, and the professional cook knew how to improvise when an important ingredient was not at hand. Indeed, many of the medieval cookery books offer alternatives for a particular dish, such as cabbage, or suggest ways of enhancing it with spices or other ingredients. The cook had to be prepared for a surprise and to be flexible as unexpected gifts of food were not uncommon. Far more was expected of a cook who served a royal master than from one employed in a less exalted household, and the hours were long and demanding. The head cook was responsible for producing a feast on a certain date, for a certain occasion, but had no control over last-minute changes of plan made by his superiors who had little or no interest in how he solved any particular problem.[13]

The master cook learned his skills through an apprenticeship and moved up the ladder from apprentice to journeyman to master. Once finished with his training, he could be self-employed, perhaps roasting meats and selling them to the public at large, or he might work for another master, or he might enter the employ of a wealthy middle-class or noble person. Only by securing work in a noble household did the master cook have any chance at all of enjoying any sort of status, and he would have had a battery of servants to assist him as well. On the other hand, in a middle-class household, the cook (male or perhaps female) dished out and served whatever he or she had produced and likely worked alone or with minimal assistance in the kitchen.[14] This was certainly the case in the Datini household, as we will see later in this chapter.

With the exception of Johannes Bockenheim, the master cook to Pope Martin V, most cookery book writers were anonymous, and we do not really know who they were or who employed them. However, Terence Scully writes of the author of the Neapolitan recipe collection that he may have been

a chief cook or he may be a *maestro della casa* of some important estate, but he shows that he is especially aware of the professional obligations that bear upon him. In several places the cook warned in very stern language to be *discreto*. The professional cook must be devoted wholly to the service of his master; he has one capital rule and that must be always to work to satisfy the master's tastes. His profession must exist solely to serve that taste. As our author writes at the end of Recipe 186, 'Fa ch'el coocho sia un ghiotto, ma non per se ma per lo suo patrone:' Let the cook be a gourmand, not for his own sake but for that of his master.[15]

The Kitchen Brigade

While we have already noted that the overall authority in the kitchen and elsewhere in an upper-class household was the housemaster, followed by the head steward who was in charge of the entire production of meals, from supplies to service supervising the head cook, the actual tasks carried out in the kitchen were divided among the staff from the roasting cook, perhaps with an assistant, who was in charge of roasting, to the person who took care of the pots and dishes (see Figures 1.1, 2.1, and 2.2). Everyone had his own specific duties and assignments; the undercook, for example, could be responsible for the completion of a dish such as a boiled meat or stew, whereas an apprentice learned how to dress meats and prepare dough. The sauce maker with assistants simmered the sauces, as well as managed reserves of verjuice, of vinegar, and of salt; he also spread the kitchen buffet with cloth and set out the dishes on it. The pottager peered into pots of potage (a type of stew or stew-soup) and another worker manned the mortar and pestle. One individual was responsible for making blancmange. The spicer (pharmacist) dispensed any and all medicines, composed the spiced wine, and provided the comfit box of spiced candy. He maintained a supply of spices for the kitchen, but it was the cook who was responsible for rendering accounts for all those spices, including sugar, purchased for any household use. There were knife sharpeners and dishwashers, who scrubbed and drew water, workers who brought in firewood, and distributors who delivered supplies. There were fire-tenders and door keepers who guarded the valuable stocks of foodstuffs. Cleanliness and health of the entire staff, from head cook to scullery hands, was essential. A good 50 percent of the personnel in any kitchen functioned as scullions, laboring in the unglamorous tasks related to cleaning. Throughout any extensive meal or banquet, they were kept busy scrubbing or hauling water, if no piped in supply was available.

Figure 2.1 Kitchen Preparation, detail of Luttrell Psalter (1335–1340), MS 42130, fol. 207v. British Library, London, UK. Source: Commons.Wikimedia.org.

They could be unpaid apprentices who performed these menial tasks as well as cleaning fish and turning spits.[16]

Some elite households had more than one steward and cook. Ludovico il Moro, the duke of Milan, for example, had four cooks: in addition to his own personal cook, there was the head cook who was ranked above the other three cooks; a household cook, who provided the meals for the staff and courtiers; and a cook for guests and visitors. Each cook had his own kitchen and staff.[17] At Urbino, Duke Federico da Montefeltro (1444–1482) employed several stewards including his personal steward, head steward, and one for guests; the head steward supervised the kitchen during food preparation, making sure dishes were to the duke's taste, and he oversaw table service. Montefeltro had his own personal cook as well as at least one other, and there was a carver, staff who brought the food from the kitchen to the table, a *credenziero* or credenza steward who prepared and served cold dishes (initially, he was a taster, that is he tasted the food before serving the master as a precaution against poisoning), and other staff to attend to his table including pages, who came from lesser relatives' households to serve at court.[18] In about 1425, Enrique of Aragon, Marque of Villena (1384–1434) wrote *Arte Asoria*, a handbook on carving for the table,

Figure 2.2 Roasting Meat on a Spit, detail of Luttrell Psalter (1335–1340), MS 42130, fol. 206v. British Library, London, UK. Source: Commons.Wikimedia.org.

which was dedicated to Felipe-Benico Navarro.[19] Though for the Spanish court, there is some relevance here as he goes into fine detail as to how every last thing should be carved from small birds to fruits and meat—it is, for Enrique, a fine art, and he also details the pitfalls of bad carving. The carving, of course, was done before the king and therefore was a performance that required the utmost skill. As well, Enrique considers manners, cleanliness, and appearance of those attending to the table and those attending the event.

Sometimes grand events like that of Giovanni Novello Panciatichi's nomination to *cavaliere* in April 1388 (see chapter 5 for an in-depth look) required even more complex staffing.[20] Two stewards, both named in the document, oversaw and coordinated every last detail including the lodging of guests and their horses; the acquisition of all that was needed for cooking; serving all the meals, including not just food, but also everything for the table service; the location of each of the banquets, as some attending ate separately from the more esteemed guests; overseeing the cooks and their assistants and everything that went on in the kitchens; hiring musicians, buffoons, and servers; hiring people to attend to the needs of the guests and the jousters; and in general, making sure that everything ran smoothly and without a hitch.

Now that we have an idea of what each staff member was required to do in a large upscale kitchen, let's see how many people it might take to prepare a complex recipe like the one for *Torta Parmigiana* (see Appendix I and II) that we have already encountered as we read through the recipe to see how the food is prepared and cooked. Looking at the Tuscan writer's version of the recipe, our kitchen brigade would include at least two or three people to do all the dismembering, chopping, pulverizing, and slicing of the chicken, onions, herbs, spices, and proscuitto crudo, and to grate the cheese; someone to make the chicken broth; someone to make the sausage; one or two people to make the filling for three different kinds of ravioli; another to make the dough; another to make the crust for the torta itself; and another to maintain the fire and watch over the torta as it baked; as well as a scullery boy to wash up, to haul wood, and do other mundane tasks. The work, then, would have been divided among specialists who were in turn assisted by other obedient helpers, and they would do the same type of work everyday.[21] To pull off this dish would take a number of people given the wide range of preparations, say anywhere from eight to ten people depending on how many tortes were to be made.

What kind of staff, if any, would there be in the average middle-class kitchen on an ordinary day? Likely it would be a woman working alone, with her daughters, or perhaps with a servant or two. She would be able to do it all, though the cooking would be on a far more limited scale than in a professional kitchen. Besides the actual preparation of food, she was in charge of household supplies of wood and water. And no one paid her overtime when, knife in hand, she disjointed or boned a chicken that she had just plucked, skinned a hare or an eel, emptied and cleaned a length of entrails to make sausage, or scalded a piglet to remove fine hairs from its skin in preparation for roasting.[22] Let's take a look into the Datini kitchen and see how it was staffed in comparison to the elite kitchen.

The Datini Cook or Women in the Kitchen

At Prato, Margherita Datini was the head of the household when Francesco was away in Pisa or Florence looking after his business interests; he was absent from Prato for weeks at a time, though Margherita joined him occasionally. Once again, their letters enlighten us. Francesco's letters were full of instructions, but he trusted her judgement, "And whatever I may have said, do what you yourself think best and I shall always be satisfied."[23] Her role was that of housemaster, head steward, and cook, and her household consisted of twenty-four "mouths," including servants, slaves, Ginevra (Francesco's illegitimate daughter, whom they adopted), Tina (Margherita's niece), Francesco's business manager, various guests (such as Ser Lapo Mazzei), Francesco's notary and his family, the Florentine politician Guido del Palagio with his wife, Giovanni Panciatichi (the daughter of Messer), and at any given time various family members such as her brother, Bartolomeo, who stayed for weeks at a time. Margherita also had "day" help, women to assist with spring cleaning, the washing, and the unending baking, spinning, and weaving. Other women were hired not only for household work but also sometimes to cook for and serve workers who received a meal as part of their pay. She often referred to the female servants as "my flock of girls" and said they could not do anything without supervision.[24]

Her domestic duties increased as time passed as Francesco's fortunes grew and the size of his household increased. She ran not only the house, but its extensions: the cellar, the kitchen garden, the stable, and the mill. As well, she oversaw work at Il Palco and their other farms, including planting, harvesting, and building, so she oversaw farm workers, stable hands, and manual laborers. Margherita received a stream of workday visitors including the man who delivered the grain, and she counted out payments to manual laborers and put money in their hands, as well as making small personal loans herself to needy employees.[25] Francesco's letters give a sense of her wide and varied duties: in addition to sending the items he requested such as food and clothing, Margherita was to wash the mule's feet, have Francesco's hose made and soled, speed the sale of wine, empty and fill wine vats, send grain to the mill for grinding into flour, as well as cook or at least oversee the cooking not only for herself and her household, but also for guests such as Ser Lapo and Guido del Palagio.[26] Moreover, she was in charge of obtaining clothes for the household, herself, and Francesco, sometimes sewing it herself or sending it out to be sewn or purchasing it, and she obtained and cared for the staples for the household including grain, flour, pigeons, wine, and oil.[27] When Francesco's demands were too much for her, Margherita would respond: "I am but a woman, and alone with a pack of little girls and have no help from any. I send what I deem best,"[28] or on another occasion, "It is fifteen blessed years since I came to Prato, and I have lived as if in an Inn" (Could Margherita be referencing the fact that Francesco was the son of a tavern keeper?), and referring to the construction, both in Prato and Il Palco, she continued, "I do not think there is a single Inn keeper who runs an Inn and oversees building at the same time."[29]

Margherita clearly knew how to cook as her letter to Francesco about cooking peas shows us: she treated them as if they were fresh field peas, rather than dried ones, boiling them separately from the herbs and onions which were mashed and then added to the peas.[30] Margherita cooked often, as we will see in later chapters, and she also directed servants in how to make a dish, including both Lucia and Domenica, for example. She prepared more than just daily meals; she made verjuice and pork gelatin, and oversaw wine making. Margherita was supposed to oversee some work at Il Palco, but told Francesco that she could not: "I had the cooking done here; and as you know, someone who is cooking cannot work at anything else."[31] This private, middle-class household was run quite differently than the upscale noble household—the tasks remained essentially the same, but with a limited staff. Guido and Nanni, who was Lucia's husband, helped out with certain tasks such as the fire, fetching firewood, hauling water from the well, doing dishes, and taking care of heavy things.[32] Her letters talk about the servants who worked in the garden, gathered produce, and helped with the animals. When Francesco was away from Prato and especially when he was in Florence, Margherita sent a servant, either Lucia or Villana, to cook for him, and she sent food that was to be prepared for his meals (and sometimes it was already made for him), and she would also tell him what he should do: "I am sending you . . . a small basket with cleaned mushrooms in it. All you have to do is put them in a small saucepan," "a lot of fresh frogs gathered today toward evening, but I have cooked them so you do not have to do it," "I am sending you plenty of spinach, two bunches of leeks and two bunches of mint. . . . Have it (the spinach) fried," or "I am sending you . . . onions and herbs for a pie . . . and a basket of onions, almonds, a cheese, twelve eggs and strongly flavored herbs for omelets."[33] When Francesco was away, she also entertained and prepared meals for guests as she did for the sister of the eminent Florentine Messer Giovanni Panciatichi and his sister's family who spent the night in the palazzo. Margherita wrote to Francesco: "They stayed the night and in the morning they ate here. I tried to provide the best hospitality I could but it was not possible to do this very well because in the morning to my misfortune, all the fish smelled bad. . . . We did our best to serve them honorably with other food."[34]

Staffing a kitchen can be a complex undertaking especially in an elite, upper-class household where a wide range of tasks needed to be fulfilled everyday in addition to simply cooking a meal; yet, even a merchant's kitchen required a varied number of people to make it run properly, though who did what is not so clearly defined. As we have seen in the Datini household, any one person might do multiple tasks depending on what was required that day. Less formally organized, it was nonetheless just as efficiently run with Margherita overseeing everything, sometimes doing whatever needed to be done herself. But what were the kitchens like, either elite or merchant class or even in the peasant's house? And how were they equipped? In the next chapter, we will follow our professional cook and the Datini into their kitchens to discover just how the medieval kitchen worked.

CHAPTER 3

THE COOK AND HIS KITCHEN

With his staff in place, let's follow the cook into his kitchen: the interior, even in this upscale kitchen, is dimly lit, with only the flickering lights of the fire and candles, and smoke fills the air from the fires burning in the hearths and from the heat. It's a large space with windows along one wall and ventilation hoods over the hearths. The cook's kitchen is cramped, crowded, and noisy with the entire kitchen brigade at work preparing the master's meal at the various tables around the room. Listen as the cook shouts his orders and we hear the responses, the thump of knives as meat is hacked, vegetables chopped, spices and herbs pounded (see Figures 1.1, 2.1, and 2.2). We hear spoons clanging against cauldrons and fat sizzling in the fire as the spits of roasting meats are turned over the flame. Water runs in the sinks as dishes are washed, pots filled, food cleaned. Rolling pins make soft sounds as dough is rolled for a torta. And the smells! A mingling of aromas of burning wood, cooking food, and sweat! Imagine what the atmosphere would be like in a small cottage with a hearth in the middle of the main room that served as both a kitchen and a general living space—only a door and perhaps a small window would allow air and a bit of light into the room. What a contrast the medieval kitchen is to our modern, bright, and airy kitchens—even if we compare it to modern restaurant kitchens with all the bustle and noise!

Yet at Urbino the guidelines for staffing Duke Federico da Montefeltro's kitchen, outlined in the *Ordine e officij* that we discussed in chapter 2, gives us quite a different picture. In the chapter discussing the position of the head cook, the writer paints a picture of a grand kitchen, almost free of humidity, with smaller spaces for the preparation of meat and fish, others for washing and polishing of silver, and for storing the service utensils. One smaller kitchenette existed solely for the preparation of the duke's meals while other areas serviced the wider household and guests. The priority of the head cook was to keep every part of the kitchen clean.[1]

But what is in this kitchen besides the hearths, sinks, tables, and people? Is there an oven for baking pastries or bread? How is everything arranged, and how does this kitchen contrast to a middle-class kitchen like that of Francesco Datini, whom we met in chapter 1, or even to a cottage? How were these kitchens equipped? These are the questions this chapter seeks to answer, and the cook himself is a major source of information as he writes his recipes from memory, whether it be the anonymous Tuscan, the anonymous Venetian, or Johannes Bochenheim.[2] We could take one recipe such as the *Torta Parmigiana* (see Appendix I and II) we have already encountered in previous chapters—what would the medieval cook need to prepare this elaborate dish? From cooks' recipes, household inventories, letters, and literary works like Franco Sacchetti's short stories, we can glean information about kitchen equipment, utensils, and cooking methods. Turning now to the kitchen, its location, and interior, we consider various aspects: specifically the hearth; the fuels used to keep the fire burning; the equipment, vessels, and implements used in hearth cooking (long-handled frying pans, pots with feet, cauldrons of cast iron, tripods, gridirons, ladles, knives, cleavers, and much more); and how cooking was accomplished.

The Kitchen

Upper-class kitchens were not situated close to the dining or main living areas due to the noise, smells, heat, smoke, and threat of fire associated with cooking, but they were often found up a flight of stairs on the upper floor or at the back of the building. Elite homes frequently had more than one kitchen: a large one for more public events like banquets or household meals and food preservation, and a smaller, private one located nearer the master's rooms for when he dined alone or with small groups of close friends. Usually kitchens were a room or a series of rooms spacious enough to allow anywhere from five to fifty people to work at once at their tables, sinks, mortars, and hearths. In the ideal kitchen, the main room had to be well-ventilated to provide oxygen for the flames of the fires in the fireplaces or open hearths and to allow the smoke to be carried up the chimneys on a flow of air. Stone-hooded hearths could be built in pairs against the walls of a large, high-ceilinged room with the main chimney in the center. In a large, high-ceilinged, upscale kitchen, pairs of stone-hooded hearths took up an entire wall; moreover, there could be as many as six hearths—so three walls of the kitchen were devoted to them. Large windows provided light and fresh, cooling air. Sinks were made of large, hollowed out blocks of stone and were drained to the cesspool. Smaller rooms adjoined the kitchen: a room for cold food, a larder for meats, a well-guarded spicery, a pantry, a wine cellar, and whenever possible, water was piped in from a nearby stream or canal. Cleanliness was imperative—everything had to be scoured and washed. Wide doors facilitated movement to and from the palace courtyard, the dining area, and the storage rooms, which held a variety of foodstuffs. Servers took the large platters of prepared food from the dishing-out tables and through a covered walkway to the master's table.[3] The table linens and crockery were stored in the kitchen or in the storage room adjacent to it and were taken to the dining area when it was time to set the table.

Not all elite homes had wall hearths; rather, the central location of the hearth remained useful especially if the cook installed finely adjustable grills and tripods within it to heat both small frying pans and very large cauldrons of meat and fish. The heat and smoke from the open fire filled the room, but a large vent located at the peak of the medieval kitchen's roof solved the problem, taking the smoke away. The Florentine writer Franco Sacchetti, a keen observer of everyday life, described in one of his short stories how a soldier, after a storm, entered a house and climbed the stairs finding himself in the kitchen with its blazing fire in the hearth with two steaming pots full and a spit laden with capons and partridges roasting over the fire.[4] Sacchetti's tale gives us the location of the kitchen on the upper floor and also describes a simple kitchen with a central hearth and basic cooking equipment such as pots and a spit.

When the hearth was moved against the wall, its projecting stone hood channeled some of the heat and smoke out the chimney. Over time, the hood became massive and facilitated the installation of a variety of devices to regulate the heat. A bracket or trammel let a cooking pot or kettle suspend over the fire. A system of hooks and chains allowed the cook to estimate fairly accurately how close his pot should be to the flame under it. A ratchet built into the links or hooks let him adjust the height of a heavy iron cauldron. Mounting the horizontal arm of the bracket on a vertical pivot allowed the cook to swing the pot immediately from the heat in an emergency; in addition, it was labor saving. The medieval cook used wood as his primary fuel for cooking. Recipe writers recognized the difficulties the cook faced normally even in preparing the simplest dish, and this is reflected in the recipes themselves: "Hoist the cauldron over a pretty little fire," "Set the pans on a gentle fire," or "insert the pot into bright embers." A wood fire was not easily regulated to keep an even temperature; enormous quantities of wood were required on a daily basis, even for an ordinary meal, and a cartload of wood was needed for a banquet. The cook had to keep the fires burning at just the right heat. The wood was lined up outside the kitchen door for easy access.[5]

If three walls were dedicated to the hearths, the fourth wall had at least one large window with shutters that could be opened to allow in fresh air, and bulky supplies such as food or fuel could be delivered through it. It provided natural light for those working in the kitchen. Without light from a window, the medieval cook and his assistants had only the flickering glow coming from the fires, which was sometimes supplemented by candle or torch light. The sinks were located under this large window and were a vital part of the operation of the kitchen: food was cleaned; utensils, vessels, and dishware were scoured; and cloths were laundered.[6] If water was not piped in, and most often it was not, then scullery boys hauled it in from the well in the courtyard in buckets—an endless task. After all the washing was done, the water was drained away into a cesspool, the street, or an adjoining canal (as in the case of Francesco Datini's house and kitchen in Prato). The doorway into the kitchen was often relatively narrow, and there was usually another leading out into the courtyard.

Of course, not all houses had a separate kitchen; sometimes cooking facilities were minimal and street vendors and taverns were a ready source for pre-prepared food. When cooking was done at home, it was in front of an open fire in a central hearth, the standard hearth in modest homes, and it occupied the middle of the main room's floor and provided both heat and a fire for cooking (see Figure 3.1).[7] But this was not always the case, Michele del Giogante (1387–1463), an accountant and poet, had a large kitchen in his Florentine home. It had windows that opened onto the front street, Borgo San Lorenzo, as well as the courtyard. A large fireplace was located along the wall with small windows above the canopy; wood was stored just outside the kitchen under the stairs. A pinewood staircase led from the kitchen down to the *sala* (a large, general purpose room with a fireplace); a door from his bedroom opened into the *sala*. In the kitchen, to the right of the fireplace, hung pots and pans, and there was a large shelf with sausages; other shelves held bread, kitchen utensils, and plates. The kitchen was equipped with a sink and drains. A door from the kitchen led to a covered porch and adjacent to that was a terrace with a large table and benches. His cellar held a variety of produce, with basins of olives, a basket of dishes hanging on the wall, casks of vinegar, two types of white wine in small casks adjacent to barrels, and distilled red wine in other casks alongside of the barrels. It also served as a granary. While other artisans often consumed their food in taverns and bakeries and had few designated places within their homes for cooking and eating, Michele was an exception and did a lot of entertaining. He was extremely interested in food and drink; as well, Michele obtained his bread from the local baker.[8]

One of the most important rooms in an upper-class household was the baker's oven, a separate room from the main kitchen—far more important than just a source of breads, including several grades of table bread and trencher bread. The room with its deep ovens and fire chambers was not only the domain of the baker, but also the pastry cook who made pies, tarts, turnovers—anything encased in dough and either baked or deep fried. The filling was made in the kitchen by the cook and then sent to the pastry cook.[9] The medieval oven was a stone cavern heated by a fire within it; when the stones of the structure were hot enough, the burned wood was removed and the food to be baked

Figure 3.1 Middle-Class Kitchen, miniature from *Tacuunum Sanitatis*, fourteenth century, facsimile of the original, P. Pazzini, E. Pirani, and M. Salmi, eds., Rome: Franco Maria Ricci, 1970. Source: Photo courtesy of the author.

inserted where the fire had been (not unlike the modern wood-fired oven). Only large establishments had their own ovens. While not all medieval, wealthy households baked their own bread (recipe collections rarely, if ever, mention making bread, it was a basic staple and not the domain of the kitchen), they did have the facility for baking all the pastries, both sweet and savory, and pies that the cooks turned out.[10] The pastries and pies could be placed in a "testo," a terracotta dome that could be placed in the hearth and covered with embers; alternatively, a brick or stone could be placed underneath the dish with another on top and then pushed into the embers. Bread was generally mixed, kneaded, and shaped at home, then sent out for baking. Pies and sometimes meat dishes were also cooked in the baker's oven.[11] In one of Franco Sacchetti's short stories, for example, Noddio d'Andrea sent three different earthenware baking dishes ("tegame") to his local baker, each filled with a variety of savory ingredients, including roasted meats.[12] For an example of a communal oven, see Figure 3.2.

At Prato, Margherita Datini had her servant Lucia make the bread from their own flour; there was a special space in the upstairs granary for bread making, with all the necessary equipment, including a madia (a chest for mixing and kneading the bread, which also served as a storage vessel), tables, cloths to cover the bread while it rose, and baskets and large sacks for the finished bread. The bread was baked at home in their "forno" (oven), located across the street in the walled garden, next to the loggia (see Figures 3.3 and 3.4 for examples of bread ovens).[13] Enough bread had to be prepared to send to her husband Francesco (in Florence) in addition to the bread they ate in Prato. Her letters to Francesco are filled with references to bread, its quality, and how much she was sending him when he was away from Prato. In her March 21, 1397, letter to Francesco, for example, Margherita wrote: "The bread is a bit darker than it was last time because it is better cooked and it

Figure 3.2 Baking in the Communal Oven, miniature from *Tacuunum Sanitatis*, fourteenth century, facsimile of the original, P. Pazzini, E. Pirani, and M. Salmi, eds., Rome: Franco Maria Ricci, 1970. Source: Photo courtesy of the author.

seems to me more healthy well-cooked than underdone."[14] The bread varied in quality depending on whether it was for their own consumption (white, high-quality flour) or for the servants (a coarser variety of mixed flours). She wrote: "Argomento will come tomorrow morning, and I will get him to bring a basket containing sixteen white loaves and six of the other kind we use for the household."[15] And on another occasion it seems that Francesco had to be satisfied with ordinary bread, Margherita wrote: "I have not baked any white bread today. . . . I am sending you some of the bread we eat because it is fine for Fattorino and the others there. Of the [twenty-five] loaves, [three] are like the ones I sent you the other time. I will have some white bread made for you tomorrow."[16] And sometimes he complained to his wife if the bread was too heavy because it was made with the coarser flour meant only for servants' loaves: "Bid Nanni take a sack to the miller and say it serves for making bread for me . . . wherefore he must grind it as fine as he can."[17] Feeding her servants was a preoccupation of Margherita's and sometimes she would not send him any bread at all, keeping what was on hand for the household.[18] Throughout their marriage, Francesco and Margherita frequently discussed, in their letters, the wheat that was harvested from their own farms, how it was to be milled into flour,

Figure 3.3 Baking Bread, detail of the Decretals of Gregory IX. Royal, 10EIV, fol. 145r. British Library, London, UK. Source: Commons.Wikimedia.org.

Figure 3.4 Baking Bread, detail of the Decretals of Gregory IX. Royal, 10EIV, fol. 145v. British Library, London, UK. Source: Commons.Wikimedia.org.

the bread that was produced from it and its quality, and how much and which kind of bread she was to send him—some aspect of bread and its making was a constant in their correspondence.

Kitchen Equipment

Recipes, by implication, tell us what sort of furniture was in the kitchen—if you were chopping vegetables, for example, you'd certainly need a table on which to complete that task, and there would have to be storage chests or cupboards for the various ingredients required to make the dish, such as jars of spices and dried herbs or wooden barrels for salt, sugar, or vinegar, not to mention places to store perishables like meats, cheeses, and fish. Occasionally, the writer does specify furniture as the anonymous Tuscan did in his recipe for stuffed lamb shoulder: "take the meat and beat it ("battile") with a knife on the table."[19] Household inventories, like those of the Datini family, expand on what the recipes tell us by noting, in their case, three trestle tables (one was made of walnut), two benches, barrels of sugar and salt, chests that held dry meats, and jars of spices, raisins, or dried figs.[20] As well, both recipes and household inventories inform us about the equipment needed to prepare a meal whether the cook, writing his recipe, specified a pot, pan, or knife, as our anonymous Tuscan wrote in his recipe for tortelli: "cook them in a pan ('padella') with lard and with oil,"[21] or suggested implements by his description of the process as in the Tuscan cook's recipe for stuffed lamb shoulder: "take a good quantity of aromatic herbs and pound ('peste') them with spices and saffron"—would this not imply the use of a mortar and pestle?[22] Household inventories list for us various objects in the kitchen and storage rooms; often, as in the case of the Datini family, the items listed are very specific: a stone mortar for making "salsa" (sauce), a copper basin for making comfits, or a copper pot to collect fat under roasts as they turn on a spit.[23] Literary works, like the short stories of Franco Sacchetti or of Gentile Sermini, also add to our knowledge of equipping the medieval kitchen: recall Sacchetti's kitchen mentioned earlier in this chapter with pots and a spit.[24]

The most common cooking vessels and utensils included a cauldron and a cast iron or copper pot for the preparation of soups, meats, and vegetables (see Figures 3.5 and 3.6). The pot on a tripod was an indispensable implement when preparing meat, especially in peasant households as they did not usually own skewers, gridirons, or other appliances for cooking on an open fire. Iron tripods came in all sizes, and there were trivets to set over or in glowing embers. Some iron braising pans had short feet so that they could be set directly into the embers of the fire, and some andirons were topped with small metal baskets designed to hold a small quantity of coals under a pot or pan—this was one way to keep food warm. There were knives for carving, chopping, and boning; slender pronged roasting forks; skimming spoons; bowls; and basins. Large kitchens were equipped with several frying pans. Long-handled frying pans and pots with feet were common and practical appliances when cooking over an open flame. For roasting meats and fish, the cook had a variety of spits and grills, depending on the size and weight of the product. Other important items included rolling pins, graters, mortar and pestles, sieves and straining cloths, colanders, ladles, huge cleavers placed on butcher-block-like tables, cutting boards, kettles, huge stirring spoons, slotted spoons, wooden spoons, scissors, tongs, rasps, and oven-shovels—all in a wide variety of sizes and types—these were the everyday working equipment of a respectable aristocratic and middle-class kitchen.[25]

Figure 3.5 Bartolomeo Scappi, Various Utensils, from *The Opera of Bartolomeo Scappi* (1570) *L'arte et prudenza d'un maestro cuoco*, translated by and with commentary by Terrance Scully, plate 10, p. 645. Source: Photo courtesy of the author.

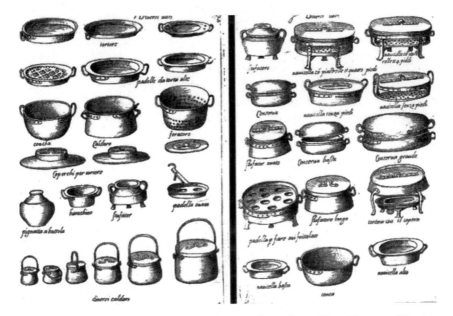

Figure 3.6 Bartolomeo Scappi, Various Pots, from *The Opera of Barto-lomeo Scappi* (1570) *L'arte et prudenza d'un maestro cuoco*, translated by and with commentary by Terrance Scully, plate 9, p. 644. Source: Photo courtesy of the author.

Just one recipe can tell us so much about equipping the kitchen, whether in words or by implication as in the case of the anonymous Venetian's recipe for *Torta Parmigiana* (see Appendix II), which we have already encountered. While he is specific in terms of quantities of ingredients (eight pounds ["libre"] of pork, twelve fresh cheeses and six aged cheeses, four capons, six chickens, half a pound ["libra"] of sweet spices and herbs, and twenty-four eggs) and how they are prepared, he never mentions equipment until the very end of the recipe when he states: "If you are using a copper 'testo,' you will want a small fire."[26] Yet we know that there must have been a pot because the pork was to be well-boiled and a knife to beat or pulverize the meat once cooked. The fresh cheese was mixed with eggs that were beaten—so a bowl and spoon at the very least. Mint and parsley were pulverized—presumably in a mortar and pestle—and a crust was made, so surely there was a table and a rolling pin. We could go on. The writer assumed a certain knowledge on the part of the cook as the title of his work implies: *Libro per cuoco*. It is a fascinating recipe from which we can learn so much and if we compare it to the more complex version written by the anonymous Tuscan, the latter is a little more forthcoming in terms of equipment: for example, the chicken was put into a pot ("vaso"), a knife was used to crush the herbs, a spoon was used to pour chicken broth over the pastry crust, and it was baked in a "testo."[27] But we would need another knife to cut up the chicken and a pan to fry it in and one to chop the onions and the prosciutto, a grater for grating the cheese, bowls and spoons for mixing ingredients, a mortar and pestle to smash the almonds, and at least one rolling pin and table. Not only is equipment implied in these recipes, but also furniture and storage vessels: a barrel or cask of oil for frying, large jugs of water for the pots, cupboards or chests for boxes, or jars of spices and herbs and the cheeses, especially the fresh and perishable kind and the lard, which must be stored in a cool place.

If our two *Torta* recipes do not tell us what we must use to boil our chicken in or chop our herbs with, other recipes do. In the *Liber de coquina*, in the recipe for cabbage, the greens are put into a pot ("pentola") and boiled, and his spinach is served in a bowl ("scodella") topped with spices and salt.[28] In a recipe for fava beans, they are put in "un vaso" with water to boil and served in a "scudella"; in a recipe for ravioli, the greens are first chopped with a knife and then further pulverized in a mortar with a pestle.[29] In his recipe for serving a crane, the Tuscan cook boiled it in a "caldaio" (kettle), then put it on a spit and roasted it.[30] This is just a sampling of what can be found in medieval recipes. Literary works, too, can be more forthcoming than some recipes when it comes to equipment. Gentile Sermini wrote about a parish priest who was a gourmet and who kept a cookbook in his breviary, as we have already seen.[31] His recipe for roasting eel reveals several pieces of equipment: a skewer for the chunks of skinned eel and bay leaves, a container ("una conchetta"—curved with a hinged lid to keep it closed) in which the dish was baked, and an aspic dish ("una conca da gelatina") in which it was served—and a warm cake pan ("una teglia") covered the dish to keep it warm before it was brought to the table.

The most common pots and pans noted in the recipes that actually suggest what equipment to use are a "pentola" and a "padella"; sometimes a "vaso" replaces the "padella" for frying.[32] Mortars and pestles, and sometimes knives, are commonly noted, and for serving a dish,

the "scudella" was the bowl of choice and appears in numerous recipes. Less often, spoons, spits, and grills are noted. Any cook following
these recipes certainly had to know what the appropriate equipment
was needed before making a dish. Some of the medieval terminology
we find in the recipes, the literary works like Sermini's, and in the
household inventories like those of the Datini family have more complex meaning and when translated are not always exact. For example, a
"vacello" or "vasello" can be a saucepan, a stew pot, or a casserole, and a
"vaso" a pot, a vessel, or a jar. Spellings, too, vary: "padella" or "patella,"
"scodella" or "scudella," and then there is the "testo," a terracotta dome
for baking, and the "tegame," which can be a pan or frying pan, but also
an earthenware dish for baking (as we saw in Sacchetti's story), as well
as the "tecchia," "tecchietta," "tecchini," or more commonly the "teglia," a baking pan or pie dish, and a "tagliero" can be a cutting board,
trencher board for serving a dish like the crane mentioned above, or a
trencher, made of wood or bread on which to eat a meal. Just to add to
the possibility of confusion, some recipes suggest the crust of a "torta"
be shaped like a "padella," a "teglia," or a "testo"; for example, in the
recipe for *Coppo di Uccello*, the crust is shaped like a "tegola" or "teglia,"
and in the *Torta Parmigiana*, the crust is shaped like a "teghia" or a
"padella."[33]

The Datini household inventories go beyond the recipes to tell us
about specialized equipment, suggesting that most kitchens had more
than just the common items that we have been discussing.[34] The inventory lists a special copper basin for washing bowls ("scodelle"), an earthenware bowl for aspic, a pot for rendering pork fat, a copper baking
pan for making Migliacchi (a Tuscan sweet made with millet flour and
raisins) and another made of terracotta, a pan for frying eggs, an earthenware oven ("fornello") for making rosewater, an earthenware pan for
roasting chestnuts, a basin for making comfits, a rack for drying figs,
an earthenware basin for refreshing fruit, a small cask for verjuice, a
sieve for straining "savore," a large knife to carve dried meat, two stone
mortar and pestles for making "salsa," a wooden vessel with a hinged
cover to dry meat, two large copper jars for water, several copper frying
pans, an enormous cauldron, and a great brass pot.

Certain items, like knives, were indispensable and served multiple
purposes from cutting up meat and vegetables to making a vast range

of chopped preparations: stuffing for large "surprise" creations, suck-
ling pigs or veal breasts filled with rich, aromatic mixtures, fillings for
vegetable and cheese pies, and for boning a shoulder of mutton, the
meat chopped, seasoned, and then reformed around the bone. All of
these required skill with the blade on a clean cutting board. A mortar
and pestle was used not only to pound or grind spices and herbs to
release their volatile flavor and aroma, but also almonds, bread, cooked
and raw vegetables, and even meats. Grinding had to be carried out to
perfection yielding the finest of powders and the smoothest of purees.
For example, to achieve a thick, aromatic almond milk, every drop of
essence had to be extracted from the blanched almonds, swollen from
their water bath. A filter, made of loosely woven fabric, was an essential
ally to the mortar and pestle. The strainer would clarify a turbid liquid
and make the results of the grinding process perfectly smooth as in
the case of almond milk; once filtered, it would be free of the powdery
debris of the ground almonds. Even bread, dried or grilled, and soaked
in a broth, vinegar, or verjuice was crushed and then sieved before adding as a thickener to sauces.[35] So even the most mundane or common
pieces of kitchen equipment had specific functions in the preparation
of food, a subject we will return to in the next chapter, but first we will
take a closer look at the Datini kitchens.

The Datini Kitchens

As we have already seen, the wealthy merchant Francesco Datini built
a grand palazzo or townhouse in Prato and a country villa in Palco.
Both residences were expensive according to the standards of the day;
the Prato house, for example, cost about one thousand florins—more
expensive even than many Florentine palazzi. One indication of luxury
of these two homes is the oil linen windows used in both of them.[36]
From letters between Francesco and his wife Margherita and other documents, we know that he took a particular interest in the construction
of his house in Prato, often there supervising the work.[37] The townhouse was constructed with an eye for comfort and luxury with fireplaces, water basins, and toilet cabinets in most rooms. The walls of
the rooms and the loggia were decorated with geometric designs, forest
scenes, and religious paintings. A shield with the Datini and Bandini

coat of arms hung in their bedroom. Francesco had canals constructed around the house to provide water for the kitchen garden and to drain waste water away. Once finished, the three-story townhouse had two kitchens, one above the other with the master's suite on the floor in between; both kitchens were at the back of the building and faced the street. Apparently, as worked progressed, the project was expanded and elaborated with Francesco calling the house "un paradiso."[38]

Begun first, the ground floor kitchen was large and its size suggests that it was meant to be a principle element in the palazzo; it was a priority for Francesco in terms of the overall building.[39] Francesco knew that this kitchen had to be large and with a hearth large enough to accommodate such tasks as rendering pork fat, making pork jelly and verjuice, washing vats for wine making, and doing the laundry, as well as for cooking meals for themselves, their servants, and guests. Both Francesco and Margherita knew how to accomplish these varied tasks, as we will see in chapter 4. Francesco took a special interest in this kitchen, in part because of his knowledge of what needed to be done there and because he loved to entertain. Next to the kitchen, the courtyard with the only well was open to the air and floors above with a graceful, protected loggia to the side. The relationship of the kitchen to the loggia meant that Francesco could easily entertain guests and if the weather did not permit eating in the loggia (inventories mention benches and tables), the "room with two beds" also functioned as a *sala* or dining room. Though not entirely completed for the 1384 Christmas celebration, it must have been functioning as Francesco hosted numerous guests, and from these documents we know that the women ate in the *sala* (referred to as "the room with two beds"), while the men were served in the loggia.[40] Again in 1393, guests were served their meal in the loggia—we will come back to these events and others in chapter 5.[41] The loggia had a dual function: when it was not being used for entertaining, utilitarian tasks such as washing and drying the vats and barrels for wine or drying meat took place here. The cantina was located in the cellar below—it too was completed and functioning by 1387.[42] It held wine from Francesco's own vineyard: Trebbiano, Vernaccia, Malvasia, and Greco.[43]

All the rooms on the ground floor were vaulted, though the kitchen did have a mezzanine or storage space in one corner of the ceiling. The high ceiling made it an airy space. The kitchen had two relatively small windows facing the street and another square window facing the inner courtyard, for light and air flow. A door led from the kitchen into the courtyard with its well, giving access to the loggia. Part of the property Francesco bought for his new townhouse included a garden, which was reduced in size as the structure grew, but enough of it remained for a kitchen or vegetable garden that Margherita oversaw, looking after plants and watering them with a pierced copper instrument.[44] In April 1394, Margherita wrote to Francesco about the garden which did not have a gate for security, and she worried about the easy access to it (and the house) through the adjoining canal that provided water for the garden. By May, a gate was in place and Margherita had a key.[45] There are remnants of a corridor and door (referred to as the "via della cucina") that led from the kitchen to via Rinaldesca giving easy access to the larger garden across the street. Crenellated walls surrounded this garden with its bench, cistern, orange trees, and terracotta pots for various plants. Francesco demolished older buildings on this site to create a vaulted cellar below ground and vaulted rooms above, one of which served as a *sala*, where in 1389 a dinner party was held to celebrate and show off this new addition.[46] The vaulted loggia with a jasmine tree overlooked the garden, and there was a coop for chickens and capons. Pigeons and peacock were also kept here. Most importantly for us was the baker's oven built for the family's needs, located next to the loggia and the walled wine press.[47] Francesco's dream was to create "a beautiful house with delicate things in which to pass the time pleasantly . . . with evenings outside in this lovely garden full of fragrant flowers of the orange trees."[48]

Located under the roof, the upstairs kitchen (completed ca. 1394) was smaller in size than the ground floor one with a lower ceiling; a small loggia opened toward the street where there was a bird bath and perches on which the pigeons slept, as well as baskets and cages for both pigeons and chickens.[49] Adjacent to the kitchen was a granary with one very small window with space and equipment for making bread. Stairs were built along the gallery of the courtyard and led from the kitchen to the floor below with an access door into Francesco's and Margherita's bedroom; in a letter of 1397, Margherita explained to Francesco how to make a dish of peas, which she said she did often in the kitchen and then ate them in the room below, perhaps in their bedroom[50] or in one of the other rooms, such as the *sala* or anterooms, any of which could be used for dining. Underneath the stair was a closet-like space for storage. The idea of the kitchen under the roof was a modification of the original plan and meant a modification in the façade (change in the windows) because of the loggia along the outer kitchen wall facing via Rinaldesca.[51]

Unlike the upscale kitchens discussed earlier, the Datini kitchens did not have adjoining specialized rooms for storage. Rather for the ground floor kitchen, according to the 1399 household inventory, storage space was found in the "room with two beds" (also the *sala*) in built-in cupboards with shelves (the outside of which was painted to match the decoration of the room) for jars of spices, herbs, and raisins; a sideboard held glasses and two handled jugs; and the loggia across from the kitchen housed barrels for wine, casks for oil and vinegar, a vat with a lid for salting dry meat, and a water basin.[52] In the room where Isoldo, Francesco's business associate, slept when he was in Prato, items were kept in another built-in cupboard: a basin for making comfits, a copper baking pan for making migliacchi, an iron grill and a pair of andirons, a mortar for spices, several baking dishes, a sack of dry roses, a jar of "olio rosato," an albarello jar of chamomile oil, and a box of rice, and the cantina in the cellar not only had wine, but casks of vinegar, verjuice, and oil as well.[53] Whereas for the upstairs kitchen, there was storage space under the stairs that held dishes, a Damascus glass cruet, silver cutlery, albarello vases, spices and a Majorca glazed basin, in the adjoining granary, and in the room where the servant Lucia slept, there was a rack for drying figs and a barrel of sugar.

In addition to the specialized items we've already discussed, in the ground floor kitchen there were a variety of other items such as a chest containing pewter plates, soup bowls, maiolica plates and bowls, both large and small, and white earthenware plates and bowls; a basin for washing bowls, another for washing feet, another for washing hands, and a large brass basin to water horses; an earthenware tub for laundry and a container of lye; knives of various sizes and a cleaver for sausages; ladles and slotted spoons; a large tripod for a cauldron that could hold three barrels of liquid; two smaller tripods; another cauldron that could hold one barrel and two more; numerous frying pans of various sizes;

andirons; graters; large and small copper pitchers; two copper bowls; two spits; a grill; a sieve; earthenware jugs for water; forms for making cheese; both large and small earthenware jars for cheese; twenty jars of oil; two barrels of vinegar; one pair of scales; a salt box; one barrel of sugar; and the list goes on.[54] The upstairs kitchen was equally well equipped: in addition to similar items as listed above, there was a chest full of already made trenchers, cutting boards, a pot for rendering pork belly, a long tripod that could hold three or four pots, a copper baking pan, large and small earthenware baking dishes, casks of vinegar, a barrel of salt, and a madia with a bucket for making bread.[55] Both kitchens had oil lamps, benches, stools, and tables.

Francesco and Margherita had some elaborate items for special occasions: albarello vases with the Datini crest, twenty-six silver forks in sheaths for their guests, two salt cellars made of walnut shells decorated with Indian silver, one large macaroni dish, and three silver macaroni forks for serving.[56] In fact in 1393, Francesco decided to buy a huge quantity of Spanish lusterware with his family crest: a shield with six stripes, three white and three red. He ordered 462 pieces on October 25, 1393, and received his order on March 29, 1395. It included, as his agent notes: "beautiful bowls, rather large ones and sauce bowls, [four] beautiful basins to wash hands and the same number of ewers . . . a few salt cellars and things you think are beautiful . . . you know who he is and that he likes beautiful things . . . and at the same time have bowls, basins, chopping boards and everything you can make with his family crest."[57]

Household inventories of the Datini are enlightening; they are more than just simply a listing of what items were in the rooms, as they can tell us about those who lived there and something about how the household functioned. This is particularly true of the 1399 inventory of the Palazzo Datini, which gives a clear sense of what was in both kitchens and how both kitchens functioned. For example, from certain items listed as in the ground floor kitchen and loggia, we know that meat was cured and salted in the loggia and stored in a chest in the kitchen, grapes were dried into raisins, grapes were pressed for wine and stored in the cantina below, horses were watered, feet washed, laundry (wash tub and that cauldron) was done, and cheese was made and stored (cheese forms and jars). The letters between Francesco and Margherita also enlighten us as to what was produced in this kitchen. In 1395, Francesco wrote that while he was at Prato and Margherita was in Florence, he had six pig haunches salted and had lard salted for roasts. Several albarello jars were filled with pork fat,[58] and later in the same year from Florence, he wrote to his wife who was now in Prato about how she should make pork jelly in a great basin.[59] Of course, Margherita wrote to her husband about food preservation, explaining to him how she had made several barrels of verjuice and also about pickling.[60] Thus not only were meals prepared in this kitchen (and served in the loggia or another room), but also larger tasks such as food preservation were also done here. The ground floor kitchen, then, was a working kitchen. Its hearth must have been quite large—at least large enough for a cauldron holding three barrels of water and its tripod.[61] It also had a large sink and a washroom and space for two servants, Nanni and Guido, to sleep; their bedding, chests, and other personal objects are listed in the 1399 inventory for the ground floor kitchen. Even after the completion of the upstairs kitchen, the lower one seems to have been the primary one serving the household of twenty-four mouths, including servants and various relatives who stayed there such as Francesco's illegitimate daughter, Ginevra, and for the completion of mundane tasks such as doing the laundry, salting and drying meat, making wine, and pickling. The upstairs kitchen seems to have been used primarily for meal preparation, for both guests and their own private meals and bread making, though its hearth must have been quite large in order to accommodate a long tripod that could hold three or four pots at the same time; moreover, chickens and pigeons were housed in its loggia.[62]

In 1390 Francesco bought a house and land at Palco and by 1393 began work on the villa, called Il Palco. It, like his townhouse in Prato, was enlarged over time. The villa had crenellated walls with a central courtyard and cistern; the ground floor rooms included a *saletta* (small, multi-purpose room), another room and antecamera or antechamber, and the kitchen with a small room next to it. The master's rooms (both a bedroom and a study) and another *saletta* were on the floor above. The villa, like the townhouse in Prato, had oil linen windows throughout.[63] As well, there was a baker's oven, a wine cellar, and a dovecote. Il Palco was meant for relaxation and pleasure, as well as functioning as a working farm, whose harvest of grain, fruit (including grapes for wine), and vegetables was sent to the house in Prato for processing. A brief inventory of the villa at Palco was taken in 1410 after Francesco's death, and of course, it included the kitchen. Though not as well-equipped as the two kitchens in Prato, it did have the basic equipment required to cook meals, even for guests, and it is likely, since this was what we might call a "vacation" house, the Datini brought from Prato whatever was needed when they came to stay. There were pewter oil lamps, tongs, tripods, pots, both large and small, a grill, a cast iron pan for frying chestnuts, maiolica bowls, ladles, pewter plates, forty-five trenchers (!), mortar and pestle, and a Bolognese wash basin.[64]

Certainly, neither of the two Datini kitchens in the Prato town-house was as large or lavish as the ideal, upscale kitchens we discussed at the beginning of this chapter. Neither one had multiple sinks or hearths, nor were there any special rooms for storing meats and cheese nor a spicery or even a pantry. Rather, cupboards in other rooms in the house served as storage space and the lower kitchen had a small mezzanine. Yet both kitchens were fully equipped just as the elite kitch-ens, suggesting to us that both Margherita and Francesco knew about cooking and what was needed, not only to make a meal, but also for food preservation and wine making. As we turn to the next chapter, we will learn about ingredients, food preservation and preparation, and cooking methods and techniques not just in the ideal world, but also in the Datini household.

CHAPTER 4

THE COOK AND HIS RESOURCES

In this chapter, we'll focus on the ingredients used by the cook to prepare a meal: spices and herbs, fruits and vegetables, meat and poultry (both domestic and wild), and fish. Often herbs and vegetables were foraged in the woods or grown in the kitchen garden. We'll look at food preservation and production: salting fish, curing meats (smoked, pickled, or dried), candying fruits and nuts, making cheese, bread, wine, olive oil, as well as cooking methods (blanching, boiling, or frying). From these ingredients, the cook could prepare stews, meat pies, vegetable torts, flans, roasts, and a variety of pastries. Recipes, like those found in the cookery books of an anonymous Tuscan or an anonymous Venetian, are not just for a specific dish, but can also explain for us the process of preserving food for later use so that we learn just how meat was cured or cheese was made.[1] Recipes, too, tell us about the resources available to a cook; in addition, poems and letters are particularly useful in detailing for us what the cook had at hand. In his series of sonnets about an imaginary court, called *Il Saporetto*, Simone Prudenzani of Orvieto, for example, wrote often about food, listing a variety of ingredients or outlining what was eaten on holidays.[2] Recipe collections themselves tell us about the availability of ingredients, how the book is laid out or how the recipes are grouped infers the significance of certain ingredients, at least on the part of the author. The *Liber de coquina*, for example, begins with vegetables, whereas the *Libro per cuoco* opens with sauces and broths.[3]

What we know about what people ate in the past reflects elite eating habits, though we can speculate to some degree about the middle- and lower-class diet. In general, roast meats were rare in the diet of the poor; it was not as common at the peasant's table as it was on the nobleman's, not so much because of the cost of the meat as it was about the practicality of cooking. A roasting fire was not the best way to conserve and use cooking heat; it required a higher heat than a stew pot, though both could be done at the same time (see Figures 1.1, 2.1, 2.2, 3.1, 3.2, 3.3, 3.4, 3.5, and 3.6). Rather, it was more efficient to keep a stew pot filled with cereal grains, vegetables, and perhaps a bit of meat than to put a roast on a spit over the flames, and of course, the stew pot was the major source of a meal for the lower classes.[4] Ironically, this so-called peasant food was not unique to them. Similar simply prepared meals were described in aristocratic cookery books: fish stew, chicken or rabbit stew, pork with peas, stewed vegetables and fruits—so a refinement of the peasant menu with the addition of veal pies, roasted and fried meats and fish, with the appropriate sauce served in a separate bowl and a variety of pasties. For the most part and with the exception of New World plants and animals yet to be discovered, the majority of foods the medieval cook received through his kitchen door were similar to those we might pick, gather, or buy today. Yet we no longer cook some species as they did such as cranes, peacocks, or small songbirds, for example. The medieval cook prepared them in a manner generally familiar to any modern cook without access to electricity or gas, though the final dishes might be quite different in terms of presentation and flavor because the cook used many more spices. Unlike today when we can buy just about anything at any time of year, what was available to the medieval cook depended on the season. Even some fish and meats were seasonal and were preserved for later use: smoked, pickled in brine, set in gelatin, salted, or dried. Fruits and nuts were candied to prolong their life. Chicken and eggs were vital staples (as they are today) and available to most people—peasants with a yard could raise the chickens and sell their eggs, for example. Spices and herbs, too, were part of the cook's repertoire, and vegetables could be grown in the kitchen garden and were also preserved for later use. As we will see, the cook had a wide range of ingredients available to him, including access to a greater range of wild species than we eat today. Once acquired, the provisions could be stored in stone jars and wooden barrels, hung in nets in the kitchen, locked in chests, or placed in boxes whose slotted sides allowed air to circulate and keep contents fresh.[5]

The Ingredients

Where did the medieval cook obtain the ingredients for his dishes? His pantry should be well stocked with spices, dried herbs, cheese, dried legumes, nuts, dried meats, and other preserved and fresh foods. The kitchen garden was another source for fresh herbs and vegetables, such as onions, garlic, greens, and legumes, depending on the size of the space. If you were lucky enough or rich enough to have a farm, then other vegetables, fruit, and grains such as barley and wheat (to be milled into flour for bread) would be readily available (see Figure 4.1). Freshwater fish could be bred in a private pond, carefully maintained on the property. Of course, the local market was a vital source for meats, poultry, fish, cheeses (see Figure 4.2), and vegetables not grown, kept, or prepared at home (Figures 4.3 and 4.4). Foraging was another option, especially for mushrooms, wild asparagus, and even frogs. Chickens, pigeons, and other fowl were often kept in cages or dovecots near the kitchen; chickens not only provided the household with eggs, but also meat. Seasonality of ingredients meant that some fruits, vegetables, and meats had to be preserved in some manner and stored in the pantry for winter use; standard in-house production included such tasks as making verjuice, drying herbs, and rendering pork fat to supplement the household stores. Recipes, again, are a vital source for us; just looking at the list of recipes in a medieval cookery book gives us an idea of what was frequently eaten. In the Tuscan writer's collection, for example, cabbage, turnips, pears, leeks, chickpeas, and peas were prepared in a variety of ways; there are also recipes for broths, for cooking cranes and capons, for making ravioli, for stuffing a lamb shoulder, for numerous tortes, fish, liver, roasted cheese, and a wide range of other dishes.[6] Health manuals, like that of the Milanese physician Maino de'Maineri give a sense of what was eaten, from cereal grains, to leafy vegetables, fruits, roots, mushrooms, meats, fish, dairy products, herb and spice mixtures, and beverages.[7] Short stories and poems also lend insights into ingredients and eating habits. In one of Simone Prudenzani's sonnets, for example, he outlines holiday eating: "lasagne of Christmas. . . spelt cakes of Carnival . . . cheese and eggs of Ascension . . . the goose of All Souls Day and maccheroni of Fat Tuesday." Another reads like the contents of a recipe book: "Tortell in a bowl and blancmange, French soup, lasagne, then ravioli followed by roast chicken," and it goes on.[8] Antonio Pucci's poem "Mercato Vecchio" tells us what could be purchased at the old market in Florence during the time of the Medici: spices, good meat, chickens, hare, boar and pheasants, eggs and cheese, herbs, and fruit.[9]

What were the most commonly used ingredients?[10] We will begin with herbs, most often grown in the kitchen garden. Parsley and sage were primarily cooking herbs and were easy to grow. Other herbs included bay or laurel, sorrel, basil, tansy, marjoram, rocket, water and garden cress, dill, and mint. But the medieval cook included with his herbs lettuces, cucumbers, cabbage, leeks, and onions.[11] Violets and rose petals were valued for their varied flavor and the color they brought to a dish and to liquids in which they were infused. Herbs and spices were generally thought of as varieties of drugs, and this included sugar. These spices, imported from foreign lands by merchants like Francesco Datini, carried almost occult properties to the medieval way of thinking and in folklore. Because they came from faraway places, spices were expensive. Pepper was the king of spices throughout the fourteenth

Figure 4.1 Ambrogio Lorenzetti, detail of the countryside and farms from *The Allegory of Good Government*, fresco, 1338, Sala delle Pace, Palazzo Publico, Siena. Source: Commons.Wikimedia.org.

Figure 4.2 Cheese Shop, miniature from *Tacuunum Sanitatis*, fourteenth century, facsimile of the original, P. Pazzini, E. Pirani, and M. Salmi, eds., Rome: Franco Maria Ricci, 1970. Source: Photo courtesy of the author.

century and was a must have in every upscale kitchen. In fact, pepper and saffron were paired in nearly every recipe in the Tuscan writer's cookbook. As well, cinnamon and ginger were frequently paired in both savory and sweet dishes. Also at hand and ready to be ground up to release their pungent or mellow zest were cloves, nutmeg, mace, cumin, mustard seed, cardamom, caraway, and anise. Salt, too, was another seasoning ingredient used just as it is today.[12] The native Florentine Balducci Pegolotti (active 1315–1346) wrote a handbook for merchants describing a variety of foodstuffs, including spices and how to identify the best and freshest products. He noted the most common

Figure 4.3 Ambrogio Lorenzetti, detail of the city from *The Allegory of Good Government*, fresco, 1338, Sala delle Pace, Palazzo Publico, Siena. Source: Commons.Wikimedia.org.

Figure 4.4 Ambrogio Lorenzetti, detail of shops from *The Allegory of Good Government*, fresco, 1338, Sala delle Pace, Palazzo Publico, Siena. Source: Commons.Wikimedia.org.

grades and variety of spices: anise, pepper (white, black, and long—a sweet, pungent variety, highly prized), ginger (six distinct species), turmeric, cinnamon and cinnamon flowers, carnation leaves and stems, cassia buds, cassia, caraway, grains of paradise, sugars (from Cairo and Damascus: loaf sugar, powdered sugar, candied sugar, refined sugar, rose sugar, violet sugar), alum, mastic, zedoary, cloves, clove stocks, clove leaves, nutmeg, cubebs, cardamom, galingale (an aromatic rhizome of Chinese origin, reminiscent of ginger, but without the lemony aftertaste), mace, cumin, carobs, aloes, sumac, and saffron.[13] One could speculate that Francesco Datini might have used Pegolotti's handbook for his importing business, and of course, medieval cooks in affluent households would have handled many exotic spices and foodstuffs on a regular basis.

By the end of the thirteenth century and the beginning of the fourteenth, in cookery books such as the one by the anonymous Tuscan, we begin to see honey being replaced by sugar.[14] While honey was added to food, much the same way as a sauce or used as a dip for fritters, sugar became part of the basic composition of the dish, as well as providing a replacement for honey in its traditional uses. The use of either one could be left to the discretion of the cook: fava bean soup was flavored with pepper, saffron, and "honey or sugar," and the Tuscan cook emphasized the preference for sugar giving a more marginal role to honey, limiting it to fritters and some desserts. Sugar also became a major feature in sauces: the Venetian cookery book, for example, showcases a sweet and sour sauce based on sugar, spices, and vinegar as the "perfect reinforced sauce." and "a good flavoring for every kind of roast."[15] Sugar, then, was used in much the same way as we use salt today. As well, sugar was seen as therapeutic and included in many sick dishes intended for invalids or those recuperating from a disease; therefore, it was deemed good for the healthy, especially when paired with vinegar in a sauce. Moreover, sugar was used as a preservative, particularly for almonds, pine nuts, hazelnuts, coriander, anise, and various candies.[16]

Besides the herbs discussed above, other important green vegetables used by the medieval cook included kale, celery, fennel (leaves and seeds), asparagus, spinach, cucumber, and endives, as well as broccoli, cauliflower, and gourd. Root vegetables were also commonly used:

turnips, the most common, then carrots, parsnips, beets, and radishes. Also significant to everyday cooking were fava beans, field peas, peas, and lentils.[17] Medieval cookbooks have a variety of recipes for vegetables and legumes. As we have noted, the Angevin cook's book opens with simple, straightforward recipes for cabbage, spinach, chickpeas, fava beans, and peas, as well as more elaborate variations. The Tuscan writer adds recipes for squash, leeks, and turnips.[18] Of course, vegetables were included in other recipes such as the Venetian writer's recipe for *Torte de erbe* ("Tart with Greens"), where he wrote, "Take a large quantity of greens, that is, chard, parsley, spinach, mint and [six hundred] grams of salt pork fat."[19] Mushrooms and truffles were also prized. Walnuts, hazelnuts, pistachios, chestnuts, pine nuts, and almonds were all kept on hand in larger kitchens. Almonds were the most widely used, often made into almond milk which was indispensable in medieval cooking, and almonds were made into a paste and into oil, as were many of the nuts listed here.[20] Olives, of course, were also produced, mainly for oil. The most common fruits were oranges, apples, pears, quince, peaches, plums, cherries, dates, and figs—made into compotes and jams, and candied; grapes were eaten fresh, dried into raisins, and used to make wine. Looking again at Pegolotti's handbook, he described an extensive variety of exotic foodstuffs such as quince wine, pomegranate wine, molasses, carob syrup, dates, currants, and purslane.[21]

A wide range of meats was available to the cook; the most common was pork followed by lamb and veal, as well as organs such as the head, spleen, and blood; poultry included capons, chickens, pigeons, ducks, pheasants, partridges, and some fowl we would probably not think of eating: peacocks, crane, heron, and songbirds. The most popular and common freshwater fish coming from both lakes and streams were pike, carp, trout, and eel. But other fish was eaten too: perch, bream, haddock, tench, mussels, crayfish, octopus, squid, lamprey, orata, stockfish, and sturgeon. If you did not live near enough to the sea for fresh fish, it was salted and dried. Salted herring and sardines were often imported, as was pickled tuna fish. For Lent, Francesco Datini ordered from Pisa, "Two barrels of good Palermo tonnina, very fine and perfect."[22] To this order, Pegolotti added salt sturgeon.[23] Meats and fish were prepared in a variety of ways: chicken ambrogino with dried fruit, stuffed peacock, crane that was first boiled then roasted, a fish torta made with a large tench or large eel, a trout pie, orata boiled in wine, and herring or sardines in a broth or crayfish that were boiled with salt and eaten with verjuice or vinegar.[24] Other ingredients essential to the medieval kitchen were oils and fats: olive, almond, and nut oils; pork fat rendered into strutto (melted), battuto (beaten and spreadable like modern lard) or lardo (which cannot be translated as lard—rather it is the highly fatty tissue under the skin of a pig, so a solid slab)[25]; liquids such as wine (for both drinking and cooking), verjuice, vinegar, must or wine syrup, and rosewater. If there was no verjuice, the Tuscan cook wrote: "Should there be a want of verjuice, you can use lemon juice, orange juice or rosewater"[26]; keep in mind that oranges of this period were almost as bitter as lemons. Honey, milk (sheep, goat, cow, water buffalo, and almond milk), eggs, and cheese; bread for trenchers, for loaves, and for cooking as a thickener for sauces; rice, grains (wheat, barley, and spelt), and pasta such as macaroni, vermicelli, lasagne, gnocchi, and stuffed pasta like ravioli and tortelli were also essential ingredients.

Just one ingredient could be made into so many other products. Grapes were made into wine, dried into raisins, or just eaten. Wine's byproducts include the indispensable verjuice. The Tuscan writer ends his cookery book with this recipe: "To made verjuice, take the lees of white wine, that is, the argol of white wine, grind it up, boil it with wine or water, and you will have verjuice,"[27] must or "musto cotto," a boiled wine syrup, saba or sapa (we will discuss these in detail later in this chapter), which is similar, and vinegar. Chestnuts, often part of the diet of the poor and also prized by the elite, were roasted, fried, and boiled.[28] Once dried, they were ground into flour for bread and cakes. Even one animal such as a pig had many uses; its feet and head could be made into a gelatin, which was then used in a variety of ways, its fat rendered into lard for cooking, and its meat salted and dried for later use. Pork was ground up for sausages, pies, and even stuffing for ravioli. The liver, spleen, and the rest of the offal was used for a variety of savory dishes. Milk (goat, ewe, and less often cow; buffalo milk, too) was made into butter, cream, and a variety of cheeses. Few actually drank milk as we might today, and cheese was one of the most important byproducts of milk with many varieties still made today: ricotta, cavi di latte, gioncata, hard cheese, fat cheeses, tomini, pecorino (ewe's milk), sardesco (Sardinian cheese), marzolini, provature, ravogliuoli, and Parmesan.[29] Cheese was eaten as part of a meal, but also used extensively in cooking. Fresh cheese was mixed into eggs, meat, vegetables, and fragrant herbs to make a wide variety of tortes and pasties. The Tuscan writer proposed fresh cheese ("cascio fresco") for filling meat crepes ("crispelli"), tortelli, and ravioli, as well as for stuffing a lamb shoulder that must also include "fresh cheese, well blended with a fair amount of eggs."[30] Along with chopped meat, fresh cheese should go into *Pastello Romano*, whereas the *Torta Parmingiana* should contain, in addition to fresh cheese, an equal amount of grated cheese.[31] But it could also be the star ingredient as in the medieval version of a grilled cheese: cheese was roasted on a skewer over an open fire and served on a slice of bread or placed on a board of dried pasta; the recipe ends: "and bring it to the lord."[32] Fresh cheese was ground with a mortar and pestle, whereas aged cheese was grated, but we will talk more about the process in the next section.

Food Preservation and Production

Because there was no refrigeration or freezing in the Middle Ages, cooks had to find ways to preserve foods for later uses, and they had to be vigilant about spoilage, especially meats. Animals were butchered daily in front of the butcher's stall (see Figure 4.5) so that there was no question of its freshness. The carcass, joints, or cuts of meat could be smoked, pickled in a brine, or, much more commonly, salted and dried as it was in the Datini household. In 1395, Francesco wrote from Prato to his wife, Margherita, who was in Florence, "I've had six pigs haunches salted and I've had lard salted for roasts. I've had several albarelli jars of pork fat made and I'll have another four haunches salted."[33] If he did not preserve his own meats, the cook could buy items in shops. Fish was also fermented, dried, salted, or smoked.[34] Salted meats and fish had to be de-salted before using, and the method can be found at the beginning of most cookbooks—"How to remove the salt from meat or fish"—or at the beginning of a recipe using salted meat or fish opening with a phrase directing the cook to soak or boil the piece of preserved meat or fish. Pickling in a salt brine was the standard method of preserving meats and fish, and it was widely practiced in ordinary

Figure 4.5 Butcher Shop, miniature from *Tacuunum Sanitatis*, fourteenth century, facsimile of the original, P. Pazzini, E. Pirani, and M. Salmi, eds., Rome: Franco Maria Ricci, 1970. Source: Photo courtesy of the author.

households in late fall. The product preserved was usable over a long period.

Platina tells us:

Pork meat is so moist that it cannot be preserved except with much salt . . . when a pig becomes a year old, it is fit for salting. The day before it is butchered, it is best to keep it from drinking because its flesh will be drier; then it should be salted carefully so that it will not rot or taste withered nor be damaged by worms or grubs. When you make a brine, put salt in the bottom of the pot or jar, then lay the pieces in with the skin down. The meat should remain in the jars until it absorbs the salt, then it should be hung up on a meat-rack where the smoke may penetrate it. From it you can take lard at will, ham, shoulder, sowbelly, tenderloin.[35]

Salt preserved the life of milk and butter. Animal milk was subject to a short life, but the life of its secondary products, cheese and butter, could be extended with salt in the same way it protected meats and fish from going bad. Almond milk often replaced cow's, ewe's, and goat's milk in medieval cookery because of its durable qualities, and almond butter, churned from almond milk, appears in some recipes. But heavily salted butter could be kept for a comparatively long time. Recipes explain how to remove the salt from butter: "To take the salt out of butter, put it in a bowl on the fire to melt and the salt will precipitate out of it to the bottom of the bowl (which salt is good in a pottage) and the rest of the butter will remain sweet. Otherwise, put your salt butter in fresh, sweet water and knead and rub it there with your hands and the salt will remain in the water."[36]

Short-term preservation methods included, the simplest of all, the pie (torta) when its crust was sealed and the use of gelatin, which performed a similar service as salt. The nature of gelatin is dry, and natural gelatin came from sheep's and pig's feet. Added to stewed meats, especially pork and chicken, it prolonged life. Fish whose skin had a mucous coating, rich in protein, such as pike, perch, tench, carp, eel, and lamprey could also be used to make gelatin. The fish with its skin was boiled and then finely strained and then pieces or fillets of other cooked fish were immersed in the resulting gelatinous liquid and the mixture was cooled and allowed to set—this gelatin would retard spoilage for a useful period of time. Spices also played a role in this preservation process essentially identical to what salt did to meat and fish. Spices with a warm and dry nature were added to the gelatin and the flesh was soaked in the mixture; let to set, it completely incased the flesh. Fresh meat and fish with a high oil content was saturated with wood smoke—smoked ham, for example; anchovies and sardines were also smoked.[37] It was not just households in which foods were preserved for later use. Because of the uncertainties of when a meal might be served, inn keepers and tavern owners had to offer dishes that could be prepared with preserved ingredients or items that were ready to serve, such as the Tuscan writer's recipe for "Jellied Fish without Oil" (*Gelatina di Pesce sensa oglio*): "Boil wine with vinegar and put in the well-washed fish to cook; and when they are cooked, remove them and put them in another container. And into the wine and vinegar put onions sliced crosswise and boil it long enough to reduce by two thirds then put in saffron, cumin and pepper and pour it over the cooked fish and leave it to cool."[38] This method both preserves and cooks the fish, whatever kind it may be, and chicken can be substituted. Maestro Martino used a different technique in his recipe for "Marinated Trout in Carpione" (*Carpionar trutte al modo di carpione*): "To prepare carpione of trout as you would a carp, clean the trout well and gut them, then pierce them in many places all over with the point of a knife. Then make a brine with equal parts water and vinegar, adding plenty of salt which you must dissolve thoroughly; and put the trout in for half day or more. And when this is done, transfer them to the table, putting them under a weight for three to four hours, and fry them well in plenty of good oil, so that they are nicely cooked but not burnt, you can keep these trout for a month, refrying them if you like, and preparing them again as you would a carp."[39]

Fruits and nuts were often candied to prolong their life.[40] They were regularly preserved in either sugar or honey, just as they are today. Sugar had two advantages in terms of preservation: durability, and it did not corrupt other foods or become corrupt and when it was liquefied. The fineness of the particles mixed intimately with other foods and bonded closely to them. Platina, once again, explains: "By melting (sugar) we make almonds (softened and cleaned in water), pine-nuts, hazelnuts, coriander, anise, cinnamon and many other things into candies. The quality of sugar then almost crosses over into the qualities of those things to which it clings in the preparation."[41] Sweet wine was boiled until most of its liquid evaporated, until it became a syrup, usually called "sapa" or "musto cotto"; it coated and permeated food, warming and drying its completion. Honey was the original preservative for this procedure. Sugar, honey, or rich red wine syrup all formed a thick syrup proven to conserve fruits (comfits) or nuts or if hardened to candy them.[42] One of the simplest preservation methods was drying, and a variety of herbs and vegetables were dried for later use, including mushrooms; vegetables were also pickled.

Many of the products discussed above were made in-house, such as almond milk, butter, verjuice, vinegar, cooked wine syrup ("musto cotto" or "sapa"), pork gelatin, rosewater made from distilled rose petals, cheese, and sausages, which were among the most popular foods, even for the poor (see Figures 4.6 and 4.7). They were bought ready-made or prepared in private kitchens. In Italy sausage was made of pork, veal, liver, lamb, and even fish. It was stuffed into an intestine and fat, cheese, herbs, and spices were added. "Musto cotto" was made by taking "new must and boiling it until it was reduced by two thirds, watching so that it does not smoke. Add crushed mustard seeds and mix well. Pour into cask and it will last four months. It can be used with pork, salted tench and to make 'mostazoli' [a type of biscotti with a must base], and in many other dishes."[43] As we have already seen in this chapter, the Datini salted pork haunches for later use and also produced such delicacies as pork gelatin. In 1395, Francesco instructed Margherita, "You should prepare tomorrow a great basin of pork gelatin . . . be well made and stiff."[44] As well, they smoked their own hams and made their own sausages and verjuice, among other products, which we will discuss next.

The Datini and Their Resources

Francesco Datini was clearly wealthy enough to own several farms (Il Palco, La Chiusura, and Filettole) that supplied his household with a

Figure 4.6 Jehan de Grise and Workshop, Cooks at Work, detail from *The Romance of Alexander* (1338–1344), MS Bodl. 246, fol. 170v, Bodleian Library, Oxford University, Oxford, UK. Source: Commons.Wikimedia .org.

Figure 4.7 Making Cheese, miniature from *Tacuunum Sanitatis*, fourteenth century, facsimile of the original, P. Pazzini, E. Pirani, and M. Salmi, eds., Rome: Franco Maria Ricci, 1970. Source: Photo courtesy of the author.

variety of foodstuffs. He had olive groves and vineyards; almond, walnut, and fig trees were grown among the vines and olive trees on the hillside. As well, his farms supplied him with eggs, vegetables, capons, and game, though he purchased veal, pork, mutton, and fish. His bread was good country bread, made of flour from his own wheat and baked at home. His favorite cheese came from Parma, his eels from the lagoons of Comacchio, his tench and pike from the Bisenzio river or the Arno. He traded with the Mediterranean region and his imports into Genoa included rice, almonds, and dates from Valencia; raisins and figs from Malaga in southern Spain; apples and sardines from Marsailles; olive oil from Catalonia and Gaeta in southern Italy; and, of course, a variety of spices.[45] At Prato, his garden yielded his favorite fruit, oranges (he selected the trees himself), and from his kitchen garden onions, garlic, mint, stonewart, thyme, marjoram, rosemary, fava beans (according to Ser Lapo, who begged a sack of them, "they melt before they even touch the fire"[46]), and chickpeas, which Francesco told Margherita through their servant Nanni de Lucca to soak all night before cooking.[47]

Margherita's letters to Francesco outlined what she was sending to him that day (mostly items he requested), offering another view of what foods they preferred and kept on hand. In addition to homemade bread, which she sent almost daily, Margherita sent Francesco their own eggs; poultry, which included mostly pigeons and capons; game (peacocks, boar); cheese—especially Francesco's favorite, the fresh round sheep's cheese made at lambing time called Marzolino and Parmesan cheese— and mushrooms, in particular the small "prugnoli" that he loved. Margherita wrote: "some mushrooms (prugnoli) . . . and don't be surprised if they are cleaned because I intended to cook them. Make sure you eat them, because they were very expensive,"[48] and in another letter, "there is a small basket with cleaned mushrooms in it. All you have to do is put them in a small saucepan."[49] She also sent him frogs: "a lot of fresh frogs, gathered today toward evening, but I have cooked them, so you don't have to do it."[50] A variety of vegetables, fruits, nuts, and legumes were also sent: "a half quart of chickpeas, a half quart of peas, a half quart of beans, a good quantity of capers, a quart of chestnuts, plenty of figs, a jar of raisins," as well as oranges, apples, pears, Morello cherries, hazelnuts, walnuts, almonds, salad greens and spinach, fava beans and field peas, leeks and mint, a jar of grapes, onions, and other "strong" herbs,[51] as well as house-made products like pickled eels, quince jam, vegetable jams (especially one made with turnips), sausages, and cured meats.[52]

They grew most of their vegetables and some fruits (oranges, figs, and grapes), but bought most of their meat and fish; foraged for mushrooms and frogs; and raised chickens, capons, and pigeons, a favorite food more prized than chickens.[53] What they didn't grow or raise was purchased from the market at Pisa, though their fish usually came from Genoa. As to be expected their diet was rich in meat: veal, pork, goat, kid, and mutton—goat dominated spring, especially around Easter, and pork was common in their diet in winter, particularly pork loin. The liver, spleen, and rest of the offal were ingredients for several straightforward and tasty dishes; pork haunches were salted for later use. Both of them were fond of veal, and Francesco purchased the best. Writing to Nanni di Lucca, he stated, "And bid Margherita to put it (the veal) on the fire in the saucepan wherein I cooked it last time and to take off the scum."[54] Francesco sent Margherita "three pieces of the veal . . . send one piece, the best, to the Podesta's wife, and tell her I could not have another, for the 'Signori' would have as much as they pleased . . . and the last piece do what you will; me thinks you would do well to invite Mess. Piero di Giunta and Mona Simona, Barzalone and Nicolo and make fine dish of herbs and eat in company."[55] Margherita wrote back, "This morning Bartolomeo (her brother), Nicolo dell'Ammanato and Tengo Buondelmonti dined with me. We ate the veal you sent us. We did not eat the omelets with herbs or drink the Malvasia wine. We had plenty to eat and there was some left over."[56] On the occasion of hosting the wife and daughter of Guido del Palagio at Prato, Francesco wrote to Margherita requesting "a roast of [twelve[capons and two kids . . . roast pork and salad."[57]

Francesco's account books are also revealing; from the poulter's he ordered capons and guinea fowl, peacocks (a great delicacy), geese, ducks, and turtle doves. Wild game such as venison, boar, hare, pheasants, and partridges were sometimes caught on their own lands, purchased, or received from friends, and at least once in a letter to Francesco, Margherita showed some anxiety over how to deal with "a very fine and big deer" presented to her husband while he was in Florence and she in Prato.[58] They enjoyed freshwater fish, especially tench, pike, and eel, as well as salted fish: trout, tuna, and herring. In fact according to Francesco, Margherita was a "salted fish lover."[59] Francesco's 1406 apothecary bill from Filippo di Lapo e Campagni, Speziali tells us that he ordered sugar, but the larger part of the bill was for saffron, pepper, ginger, cinnamon, clove, nutmeg, cassia, and ganingal.[60] In a letter to Francesco, Margherita outlined the contents of a missing chest mentioning spices, but more specifically, ginger, saffron, rice, and a jar half full of green ginger.[61] Also in the larder were bread, lasagne, vermicelli, and "minudetti," a dried pasta in various shapes, cooked in liquid broth to make a soup.[62] In addition to Parmagiano and Marzolino, they also preferred cheeses from Craponne, Kandazzo, and fresh Pisa cheese.

Household inventories and letters tell us about in-house production at Palazzo Datini. Margherita had eels pickled in their own fat with strong spices and wine,[63] made pork gelatin adding candied peel for color and made from pig's head and feet,[64] and salted pork already noted in a letter from Francesco to Margherita and suggested by the vat for salting meat and the wooden box with hinges for storing dried meat noted in the 1399 inventory.[65] As well, they made their own prosciutto, pork sausages and mortadella, and quince and vegetable jams, particularly one made with turnips—in an undated letter from Francesco to Margherita, he tells her to make plenty of them, for he remembered enjoying them as a boy: "Monna Piera was wont to make good ones of turnips."[66] A rack for drying figs and Margherita's letter to Francesco stated that she sent Guido to their garden at La Chiusura to collect figs for drying, suggesting another house made product.[67] Herbs were dried and kept in albarello jars. [68] Cheese forms and earthenware jars for cheese attest to household cheesemaking.[69] In a letter to Francesco, Margherita wrote, "The verjuice has been made and we have filled the small barrel [probably the one noted in the 1399 inventory] . . . and we have filled a large barrel that Francesca sent me to fill. . . . Send me a barrel and I can fill it."[70] Not only was a special pot for making sapa, the rich, spiced wine syrup, noted among the various items in the 1399 inventory, but Francesco wrote "and pears cooked in sapa"[71] and rosewater was made in an earthenware "fornello" from a sack of dried roses kept in a cupboard in the room where Stoldo slept along with jars of "oglio rosato" and "olio di chamomilla."[72] Finally, in the loggia of the Palazzo at Prato there were vats and barrels for wine, which Margherita had cleaned and dried on trestles in preparation for wine making.[73] The press was in the garden across the street. The grapes for the wine came from the vineyards at Palco and Filettole. They were gathered and then brought to Prato for processing. Barzalone, their "fattore," had special skills when it came to making wine, though Francesco sometimes had professional tasters come in and of course both Francesco and Margherita expressed their opinions. They sold the best wine, though some was kept for company.[74]

In many of Margherita's letters to Francesco, she included recipes or at least told him how something should be cooked and occasionally he did the same, as in his letter to Nanni di Lucca, who was to convey this message to Margherita concerning chickpeas: "They should be boiled in a little water and often stirred, that they cling not to each other as they swell. And after awhile, take a greater pan, well scoured, and pour them therein with their water and oil and salt and let them boil gently and when needful, fill up with a little more water."[75] Margherita in turn told Francesco how he should have some peas cooked, "I put them on the fire, as you do with dry chickpeas. I boil herbs and an onion in a separate saucepan, and then I beat them. When I put the peas in the larger saucepan, I put the herbs and the liquid over them as you usually do with fresh wild peas. Villana knows how to cook them because she has seen me cook them so many times that she must remember. Monna Mea has also seen me cook them. She and I cooked them; she beat the herbs here in the house and thought they were very good. We ate them in the downstairs room."[76] It is clear that both Francesco and Margherita knew something about cooking and both these recipes tell us so much about cooking methods and techniques, but that is the subject of the next section.

Food Preparation Techniques

This section is about the techniques used to prepare ingredients for a particular dish, whether it is simply washing and chopping the product, making a sauce or broth for the dish, or making a dough for ravioli or a crust for a torta. It is about what happens in the kitchen once it is time to cook a meal. To begin a dish, vegetables, meats, and fish needed to be cleaned and washed, meats de-boned and fish gutted, then chopped into pieces. Before a chicken could be cooked in whatever manner, for example, it needed to be cleaned, washed, de-boned, and chopped as was done at the beginning of the recipe for *Torta Parmigiana* (see Appendix I and II). Yet even before beginning a recipe there were some not-so-pleasant tasks that needed to be done: chickens needed to be plucked, a hare or eel skinned, entrails emptied and cleaned, or a piglet scalded to remove the fine hairs—processes we rarely do today. Ingredients were chopped, pounded and pulverized, or crushed and pureed, all techniques that reduced an ingredient into pieces or pastes (see Figure 2.1). Herbs were minced, spices were crushed, eggs were beaten, and cheese was grated or mashed, depending on whether it was aged or fresh. Preserved fish and meats had to be desalted, and stuffing for pies, ravioli, or sausages made. Many ingredients were beaten with a knife

rather that mashed in a mortar with a pestle to pulverize it or the ingredient was first smashed with a knife on a table (meats and fish, usually)
and then further crushed in a mortar and pestle. Mortar and pestles of
stone, marble, or wood were used to grind herbs, spices, nuts, garlic,
cooked chicken breast, pieces of fish—any ingredient that needed to be
reduced to a powder or puree before it was entered into the dish.

Some preparation took time and required special techniques; take
pasta for example: lasagne, macaroni, or vermicelli (see Figure 4.8).
Lasagne, which were cut from a sheet of pasta dough formed with a
rolling pin, are the successor of the *lasagnae* of Roman times, called
tria; Apicus included two recipes in his fourth-century treatise.[77] Macaroni and vermicelli were common in medieval Italy, with recipes in
several cookery books. Sicilian macaroni was made of the whitest flour,
egg white, and rosewater, and the dough formed into round sticks a
hand's width in length and the thickness of straw. An iron rod was
inserted lengthwise into the dough and rolled back and forth on the
table; they were then dried in the sun and could be kept two or three
years. It took much time and patience. Roman macaroni, on the other
hand, was made by wrapping dough cut the width of a finger around
a stick, so that it stayed like a ribbon.[78] Yet an even simpler version of
macaroni or gnocchi, in the oldest meaning of the term, was made of
flour and bread crumbs and mixed with cheese or egg yolks to form
balls of dough that were cooked in boiling water.[79] Lasagne were made
fresh, never dried. In the *Liber de coquina*, the dough is made from
fermented dough, which is unique: "To make lasagne take fermented
dough and make into as thin a shape as possible. Then divide it into
squares of three fingerbreadths per side. Then take salted boiling water
and cook those lasagne in it. And when they are fully cooked add grated
cheese. . . . Then eat them by taking them up with a pointed wooden
stick."[80] What is also unusual about this recipe is the fact that the writer
explained how the lasagne were made and how they were eaten. In
other recipes, lasagne were made with flour and water, then boiled in
meat broth or in almond milk.

Making sauces and broths also took time and needed to be prepared
in advance of making the final dish. Two different sauces were common:
sapore/savore (serving sauce) and salse (cooking sauce). A very rough
distinction is made between a sapore and a salsa. A sapore is a garnish

Figure 4.8 Pasta Making, miniature from *Tacuunum Sanitatis*, fourteenth century, facsimile of the original, P. Pazzini, E. Pirani, and M. Salmi, eds., Rome: Franco Maria Ricci, 1970. Source: Photo courtesy of the author.

with which to eat the preparation; in a way, it is both supplementary and complementary to the dish. A salsa is an integral part of the dish and helps to determine the nature of the final preparation. The sapore is valued for its faculty of imparting flavor to the preparation. Boiled meats are usually cooked with a salsa; the same "broth" may serve as a sapore or serving sauce when the cooked dish is presented at the table. Savory pies (tortas) have their sapore added into them toward the end of their baking, as we see with the *Torta Parmingiana* (see Appendix I and II) where the testo is taken off and the torta bathed in the savore.[81] Roast meats usually have this sapore added just before they are served. As well, the sapore could be brought to the table in bowls for the diner to dip the meats into it.[82] And that is exactly how Sermini's *San Vincenzo's Day Roasted Eel* was served, with its savore alongside in a "concia."[83] Sometimes the sauce was too thin, so bread, dried, toasted, grilled, whole, or grated into crumbs, was added to sauces when the cook did not want to alter the delicate flavor of the spices that were combined there. A starch made of wheat or rice flour (called "amidon," the starch washed from the flour by kneading dough under water and then letting the cloudy water sit so the starch settles at the bottom) functioned in the same manner. Eggs were also used as a thickener, especially in pies, added just before finishing the dish; ground almonds could also act as a thickening agent. As well, boiling a liquid reduced and thickened it.[84]

Cooking Methods and Techniques

Food could be simmered or stewed in a large iron or copper cauldron, which might stand on its own supported legs in the heart of the fire or be suspended from a chain over the flames used to cook the basic meat and vegetable soups and stocks (see Figure 1.1). Small quantities of soup, porridge (a thick cereal, like oatmeal usually boiled in water or milk), or some drink might be heated or kept warm in a long-handled saucepan, set to stand on its own trivet beside the fire. Food could be fried in a pan, grilled on a gridiron, or turned on a spit (see Figure 2.2). Sauces, vegetable dishes, and thick slow-cooking purees were simmered in small earthenware pots. Not every household was lucky enough to have all this basic equipment on hand, nor were there full-scale ovens—rather the village oven was put to use. A small improvised oven (or a testo) could be put together and put on the fire. Food was placed on a metal plate or bake stone and covered with a lid and pushed into place with ashes piled over it.[85] Regulating the heat of the open flame was a demanding task. Pots and pans had to be kept far enough from the flames, an effort facilitated by legs and tripods supporting cookware and adjustable pot hooks, slots, and chains.[86]

Cooking over an open hearth was an all-embracing way of life. The flickering flames warmed and illuminated the room. Cooking was continual, whether flipping the contents of long-handled frying pans, swinging and stirring the pots that hung over the fire, or basting fragrant meats as they turned on the spit. Most upscale kitchens had more than one fireplace with chimneys for ventilation, as discussed earlier. One fireplace was kept burning at a low steady heat at all times for simmering broths and stews and for boiling water. Others might glow with radiant embers for grilling on a spit.[87] Skill was required to manipulate the heat of the fire and control the cooking. Sometimes this meant moving the pot to the very edge of the heat, especially for delicate dishes that were required to cook slowly, away from the smoke. For roasts, the cook had to judge the distance from the fire according to the size and quality of the meat. It was important to start at a reasonable distance so that the roast would cook thoroughly and uniformly. Then the spit was generally moved closer to the fire and turned more quickly.[88]

A variety of cooking techniques were used by the medieval cook: boiling, blanching, parboiling, and frying. Lard and olive oil could be used for both boiling and frying. Sausages, for example, were boiled, smoked, or grilled on a spit, and fish poached, fried in a cast iron or copper pan, grilled on a gridiron, or baked inside a pie or pastry shell. It was not unusual for several techniques to be used successfully for the same ingredient: browning before simmering; blanching before grilling. Wild mushrooms, for example, were parboiled before pan frying them. Green vegetables were often plunged into simmering water to set the color and remove some of their bitterness before the final preparation or cooking took place. Before roasting or any other preparation, large birds were plucked after soaking in hot water, whereas small birds were plucked dry. Meats and fish could be boiled first, ground in a mortar, then fried in lard and finally simmered in water and almond milk. Acidic liquids such as vinegar, verjuice, wine, musto, and acidic fruit juices were important to cooking. For *Chicken Ambrosino with Dried Fruit*, the chicken was first fried in fresh pork fat, then cooked further with almond milk, a little wine, and spices. It was finished with chopped dates and prunes, and grilled bread crumbs mixed with wine and vinegar.[89] Recipes often required that meats and vegetables be cooked briefly in water or a meat broth (parboiling) before undergoing the principal cooking method, whether it be frying, baking or further boiling with other ingredients. Meat could be boiled and then dipped immediately into cold water, then finally mounted on a spit and roasted. This interruption in cooking allowed the addition of other ingredients into the pot such as eggs or spices. Savory pies (tortas), also, were regularly taken out of the oven just before their time in order to have flavorings (particularly the volatile rosewater) added through the hole in the top as in this recipe for *Eel and Spinach Torta*: "And when it is half cooked, take a little verjuice and rose water, with some sugar; and make many holes in the top crust so that these things can penetrate when you put them on top."[90] Dishes could be flavored in a variety of ways with herbs, the most common were parsley, then marjoram and mint or spices: pepper and saffron, or cinnamon, ginger, and cloves. Spices were usually dispersed in a liquid—wine, verjuice, vinegar, or sour fruit juice—and strained before being added to the rest of the dish. A dish could be sweetened with must syrup ("mosto cotto" and "saba"), honey, and sugar, and garnished with sugar and/or cinnamon, sugar, and rosewater (common for tortes); pasta was garnished with cheeses and spices.[91]

Cookery books are not the only sources where we find recipes that tell us about cooking methods and techniques. Gentile Sermini's parish priest, Ser Meoccio of Pernina in Montagnold near Siena, loved good food above all else and, as we have already noted, he kept in his breviary a cookery book.[92] His recipe for *San Vincenzo's Day Roasted Eel* tells us that first we must skin the eel in boiling water, remove the innards, and cut off its head and tail, then we must wash it in six changes of water and cut it into chunks a hand's breadth each and put on a skewer with bay leaves in between each chunk to keep them from sticking together. The eel is gently roasted. At the same time, in a container salt, vinegar, and a small drop of oil are mixed with four spices (pepper, cloves, ginger, and cinnamon) and with a small branch of rosemary; the eel is basted with this mixture. Once cooked, the eel is boned and the chunks are arranged in an aspic dish ("concha da gelatina"); six pomegranates are squeezed over it, with at least twenty oranges and plenty of fine spices. Finally, it is covered with a cake pan ("una teglia") to keep it warm.[93] We learn how to prepare the eel for roasting, how to prepare the basting sauce, and how to roast and serve the eel with its "savore" on the side.

Recipes tell us how a dish could be cooked. In the *Liber de coquina*, for example, the cook explains, in his recipe for *Coppo of birds* (d'uccelli), that after the crust has been formed in the shape of a "tegola"(tile) and after the upper crust is in place, put it to cook in an oven or a testo ("metti a cuocere nel forno o nel testo").[94] While a "coppo" can be an actual baking dish (from which the dish gets its name), here it is made from dough and baked in an oven or in a testo (a terracotta dome), pushed into the embers so it is covered top and bottom.[95] Dough could be put into a particular pan or baking dish like a "tegame" or "teglia," or it could take the form of that item as we see in the recipe for the *Torta Parmingiana* (see Appendix I and II). Baking with fire above and below, in an oven, or a testo was common. The torta or pastello (tart), an invention of the Middle Ages, was a shell of dough placed in an oven or between red-hot slabs of stone or earthenware or a testo with the dual purpose of containing or cooking a filling and transporting it to the table. It was extremely practical, easy to make and to keep. The filling could be simple or complex, cheap or costly—part of a common culture both urban and rural, both elite and common.[96] A torta was eaten much the same way as an open-faced sandwich with pieces sliced off or cut into wedges like you would do with a quiche today. Torta was a basic mixture of eggs, cheese, milk, spices, fat, herbs, and greens baked slowly on a lower crust in a covered dish or on hot coals.[97]

We end this chapter with our favorite dish, the Tuscan version of the *Torta Parmigiana* (see Appendix I) as a way of summarizing all that we have discussed in terms of food preparation, cooking methods, and techniques. Let's begin prepping for this dish by cleaning, dismembering, cutting up, and frying the chicken; it will be part of our broth. As the chicken cooks, the onions need to be chopped and the herbs and spices crushed and pulverized. Once the chicken is cooked, it needs to be de-boned, the meat mixed with a beaten egg and smashed until fine, and then placed in a "vaso" (pot) to cook over the fire. Someone needs to make the dough for three different kinds of ravioli (cheese, herb, and sweet), and another person must make the stuffing for each. The almonds and dates, for example, have to be chopped and smashed for the sweet ravioli, and the cheeses either grated or smashed in a mortar and pestle. Our pork sausage mixture must be stuffed into the pork intestine and probably boiled. The prosciutto crudo needs to be chopped and the torta crust made. Finally, we are ready to layer the ingredients into the crust that is shaped like a "padella" (pan): meat first with broth spooned over, then the cheese ravioli and their "savore" and a layer of prosciutto, and it continues until all the ingredients are gone and broth is poured over, the top crust put in place and rubbed with lard. We'll bake in a hot "testo" pushed into the hot embers. Toward the end of baking, we'll have to remove it and bathe it with more broth. Can you envision what our torta must look like? One cannot help but wonder how long it would take to make all the parts, assemble them, and then bake it—hours, an all-day project. We turn next to cooking, putting all that we have learned in the previous chapters into practice.

CHAPTER 5

BRINGING THE MEAL TOGETHER

By way of conclusion, this chapter will focus on the meal. In previous chapters, we have been in the kitchen, surveying its layout and equipment (see Figures 1.1, 2.1, and 2.2); we have gathered together our staff, and we know what ingredients are available to us for creating a memorable meal. But before the cooking starts, a plan is necessary—so the professional cook in collaboration with the head steward must decide exactly what is to be served. As modern cooks, we could consult our medieval cookery books for recipes as we would today, but they do not include set menus.[1] However, not so for the medieval cook, based on past experience and training, he and the steward would plan the meal and how it was to be served. After which the hustle and bustle in the kitchen would begin as the professional cook prepares a meal, directs his staff, and oversees his kitchen. No detail can be overlooked as wood is gathered for the fire, pots filled with water, and ingredients gathered together. At the hearth, an assistant turns a spit of meat and others stir a cauldron of bubbling soup, chop vegetables, and do a number of menial tasks. Once the dishes are finished, service begins—the orchestration of the meal.

For us, unlike the professional cook who was experienced in menu planning, we will turn first to literary sources such as the short stories of Gentile Sermini (his priest explains how to cook an eel and has a plan for the menu for the San Vincenzo feast) and the poems of Simone Prudenzani, which will provide us with some insight into how meals were planned and what was served. As well, documents recording actual events like the celebrations of Giovanni Novello Panciatichi (1355–1404) in 1388 and of Sozzo Bandinello Bandinelli for his son, Francesco, in 1326 illustrate just how complex meal planning and the orchestration of dining could be. Both Giovanni Panciatichi and Francesco Bandinelli were nominated to *cavaliere*. The Panciatichi documents are a series of lists including what was to be purchased for each meal, how much of each item was needed for each guest, what staff was needed, who would attend each meal, and even what was needed for the horses. Though there are no set menus, unlike the Bandinelli documents which are exclusively menus, we can determine what was served at each of the Panciatichi meals. We will then turn to consider what it takes to serve a meal; because there was not a specific dining room as today, first the tables had to be set up, and the dishes, glasses, salt cellars, water basins, napkins, and table decorations put in place.

Finally, we will turn once again to the Datini, who hosted a wide range of guests, from illustrious men to humble employees, and a variety of events both in Prato and at Il Palco. Through their letters to each other, we know, too, that both knew how to cook and both planned menus. Though he was the son of a tavern owner, it is unlikely that Francesco, now a wealthy merchant, ever cooked for his guests, whereas we do know from her letters to her husband that Margherita, at the very least, oversaw what went on in the kitchen and sometimes assisted in the cooking of certain dishes. Francesco ordered food for various events, usually meats, such as veal, capons, or pork, and he requested certain dishes for meals, as he did for his homecoming to Prato in 1389: "one good broth with full fat cheese. . . . Fresh eggs and . . . a lot of good fish from the Bisenzio [a river], . . . lots of good figs and also some peaches and walnuts."[2]—and of course he instructed Margherita how to treat his guests when he was not present so that she brought honor to the Datini as well as her guests. When the Datini hosted a guest or guests, which they did frequently, the meals became lavish, as we will see.

Planning and Making a Meal

While the medieval cookery books are a fine source for recipes informing us about cooking techniques, equipment, and ingredients, for meal planning, Gentile Sermini's short story about Ser Meoccio, the parish priest we've met in previous chapters, tells us one way to plan a meal. Meoccio loved good food more than anything else and was also completely involved in the process of making a meal. As the story goes, he had his parishioners make offerings of food as alms to God (Meoccio, of course, acted as surrogate).[3] So the peasants, believing the priest, heaped the altar with all the produce from their gardens, their farmyards, and their flocks; on San Vincezno's day, Meoccio placed special value on these offerings as honoring the saint. That year, San Vincenzo's day fell on a Friday (January 22), and a peasant named Vincenzo delivered a beautiful eel weighing ten libre (six and a half pounds) to Meoccio's house while the priest was giving his sermon. Flustered by the gift, his cook came to the church and through gestures told Meoccio about the eel—he wondered how he was supposed to cook it. Through his sermon narrating the miracles of the saint who ate and drank in moderation, Meoccio told a story that he had witnessed—his teacher and four friends had ordered an enormous eel to be cooked. Through this tale, Meoccio explained to his cook how to prepare the eel (see chapter 4 for this recipe); as well, the priest outlined the entire menu for the feast: It started with boiled eggs, then four boiled tench with "savore bianco," a white sauce in a large bowl (scodella), then the roasted eel with "savore" (sauce) that was in the "concha," and finally a torta with lots of sugar and "confetti di anice" (anise confetti). Ser Meoccio hastened to finish his sermon in order to rush home and oversee the preparation of this magnificent feast. The six priests stuffed themselves, while the peasant Vincenzo and his family ate a meal of dried fava beans and bony little fish. Of course, this is a tale about gluttony, but it also tells us much more. It gives us a detailed recipe for roasting an eel. We know the menu and number of the courses that were served, because it was a Friday no meat was on the menu, only fish. Of course, the eel was the main attraction for this fairly typical meal.

Like Sermini, Simone Prudenzani describes a rich feast, this time at the past, imaginary court of Pierboldo, Signore of Buongoverno. As well, there is dance and music, games and hunts, a Lenten meal consisting of eight courses, and other elegant menus. For the dinner with il signore and his guests, we have a full menu: tortelli in scutella and biancomangiere (white sauce), ravioli and lasagna in broth, and soups in the

French style. There were boiled meats: chicken, pork, and boar. A rich stew of hare followed, then roast game birds: thrushes, pigeons, and partridges with vermiglio wine and orange sauce, and tartare (a kind of custard torta) and other savory meat pies.[4] The feast ended with fruit conserves of apples, walnuts and anise, cooked pears and tragea (sugared almonds), confetti, and a "good glass of wine." The sonnet that follows this one is all about the wine served at the court and another is about sweets and spices—a listing of many varieties.[5] Though these are "imaginary" meals, both Sermini and Prudenzani certainly knew about grand banquets and the types of dishes served, not only for celebrations but everyday meals as well. Actual events expand on these stories, giving us a picture of how they were staged.

Meal planning involved more than just the menu, and two different events illustrate for us just how complex it was to orchestrate a grand meal or in the case of these two, several meals over the course of several days. A series of documents for the festivities held in April 1388 celebrating Giovanni Novello Panciatichi's nomination to *cavaliere* are enlightening. The event took place on April 26 in Florence in the "tempio di S. Giovanni," the baptistery followed by several days of festivities in Pistoia, all of which had to be organized: staff hired, menus planned, food purchased, horses stabled and fed, rooms for guests found, just to name a few.[6] On the other hand, the documents for Sozzo Bandinello Bandinelli's festivities at his brilliantly assembled court in Siena in December 1326 simply outline several menus to celebrate Bandinelli's son Francesco's nomination to *cavaliere*.[7] We will focus on Giovanni Novello Panciatichi. Panciatichi came from a powerful family whose wealth came from commerce with France. A noble (magnate) of Pistoia, the title *cavaliere* was bestowed on Panciatichi by the Signoria of Florence.[8] On Monday after his nomination, Panciatichi returned to Pistoia from Florence and ate with the "signori Anziani" and other officials at his home. Later that evening, he hosted a fairly simple dinner for one hundred guests, many of whom had accompanied him to Florence including a brigade of jousters. The mid-day dinner (*desinare*) was for only nineteen people and the guests were served veal, an "arrosto" of capons, pollastri and pigeons, ravioli made of fresh cheese and tartare (a large, open-faced, custard torta), followed by confetti, whereas the evening meal did not include veal. The guests were served an array of poultry instead. The main event was the mid-day dinner for 250 people of varying status held on Tuesday, and it was followed by a light evening meal ("cena"), then a mid-day dinner and a light evening meal the next day, all with a varying number of guests and dishes.[9]

The documents for the Panciatichi celebrations include two "meal" lists, the first one notes what was to be served at each meal, a menu of sorts, whereas the second list is a plan. It outlines just how much veal or how many capons, for example, were needed for each meal: Tuesday's lunch required 625 libre of veal and 125 capons. This list is broken down into groups of guests with the amounts of veal or capons each was to be served: the men, jousters, and "signori e officiali," received a six-libre piece of veal, whereas the women, musicians, and singers received only four libre, and the workers, one libre. We learn from this list that not every guest received the same food, which is quite typical for such events, the higher the status the better the food. As well, this planning list ends with a grand total of what was needed to feed all the guests over the two days, including even the number of platters for serving the meal. Another document, which might be called a supply list, notes the ingredients for making ravioli gialli ("formaggio per ravioli," "porco per ravioli," and saffron is listed among the spices) or gelatin ("capponi per l'arrosto e gialatin"), or other cooking necessities such as lardo (solid pork fat), struto (melted pork fat), savore, spices, and eggs, but not just food (veal, pork, capons, pigeons, and so on): the dishes and platters for serving the meals, the tables and all that goes on them for a proper table setting and service, the bread and wine (white and vermiglio), and even hay and straw for the horses are also included in the planning. The next document is an outline of all the staff that was needed to host the events, cook the meals, and welcome the guests (see chapter 2 for more detail): some forty individuals, each named and given a task whether it was serving at table, assisting the cook, or working in the stable, as well as purveyors of the food or individual to provide rooms for the guests, or individuals to welcome or introduce various groups of guests, to name only a few of them. Two sinsiscalchi (chief stewards), Bartolomeo di Nieri and Sir Baldo di Mazzo, were enlisted to oversee the court, and they had assistants as well. It is of interest to note that the food served to the women was prepared in a separate kitchen ("la cucina delle donne") by Lazaro di Colino and

Nicolo di Tomeo and brought to them by two attendants, Paparino and Ciabotta. Nothing was overlooked.

Let's focus on the grand luncheon or mid-day dinner (*desinare*) held on Tuesday for 250 guests who were listed by status and gender, but not by name: "ragaionasi" "forestieri" (foreigners/guests), "cittadini" (citizens), "donne" (women, who were seated separately), "trombetti e pifferi" (trumpeters and fife players), armegiatore (jousters), among others. In preparation for the morning meal, 125 platters had to be found; enough tables and benches found and set up; and tablecloths, napkins, cutlery, serving dishes, glasses, pitchers, plates, flasks for wine, and salt cellars had to be gathered. Food had to be ordered for the meal: 625 libre of veal, 124 libre of cheese, and 125 capons. The luncheon began with "confetti dorati," white wine, and sugared almonds ("trigea"), followed by the veal, which was probably roasted on a spit and basted with a sauce, and capons, also likely roasted as they were for Wednesday night's meal; next came ravioli gialli (yellow ravioli) and cheese, and the meal ended with fresh cheese (giunchate) with sugar and cooked pears. Overall, it was a fairly straightforward and simple, yet elegant banquet.

Veal dominated each meal except for Tuesday evening when it was replaced with a range of poultry and the ravioli was replaced with "fritellette" (small fritters). Everyone, even the lowly workers, received a portion of veal when it was served at a meal, and veal was the most gifted item, nearly every donation whether it was from a guest or a nearby commune was veal, followed by wine. Gifts of food and wine were quite typical and helped to defray the cost of such events. All the meals were fairly simple in terms of preparation, but the cooks had to make ravioli to serve a total of 350 people, "fritellette" for 130, and "solcio" (shaped and marinated meat, here veal and chicken were used) made for two meals (first dinner and the last) serving two hundred total. Though bread and wine are not listed for each meal, they are included in the supply listed noted above, so certainly both were served along with the various dishes. Some dishes are missing: no savory torte or pies nor vegetable dishes were included, though tartara, a kind of custard torta made of cheese, eggs, and sugar, was served at two evening meals.[10] Even the desserts were simple: sugared almonds, fruit, or fresh cheese with sugar and cooked pears. "Trigea" or sugared almonds were served at every meal. How do the meals served by the Panciatichi compare with the Bandinelli meals?

The documents recording Sozzo Bandinello Bandinelli's events are straightforward menus. Like Panciatichi, Bandinelli, from Siena, was a rich and powerful man from a noble and ancient family with his wealth coming from commerce.[11] The festivities began on Thursday, December 18, 1326, with the culminating banquet held on Christmas Day with some four hundred guests attending including high-ranking officials: Capitano del Popolo, Camitano del Guerra, Capitano di Giudizia, the Podesta, ambassadors, and gentlemen. In all there were five banquets held over the week each with a varying number of guests and dishes. We will focus on the menu for Tuesday, December 23, but first let's look briefly at the Christmas Day meal, which was primarily meats including lots of game: boar, hare, fowl, and so on. On Christmas Eve, however, everyone was served fish—five different dishes. Tuesday's menu began with ravioli bianchi (white ravioli made with cheese not unlike those made for the *Torta Parmigiana*), boiled veal, and venison, after which the guests were served chicken ambrosino— the recipe follows. The chicken was followed by roast capon and candied pears with treggea (sugared almonds)—a constant at the Prudenzani, Panciatichi, and Datini meals. The recipe for "chicken ambrosino" follows here:

> If you want to make a chicken ambrosino, take the chickens, cut them up, then put them to fry with fresh pork fat and a bit of onion, cut crosswise. When this is half cooked, take some almond milk, mix it with broth and a little wine, and add it to the chickens, first skimming off the fat if there is too much; add cinnamon cut up with a knife and a few cloves. When it is dished up, add some prunes, whole dates, a few chopped nutmegs, and a little crumb of grilled bread, well pounded and mixed with wine and vinegar. This dish should be sweet and sour; and be sure that the dates do not burst open.[12]

The Bandinelli banquet was more elaborate than that of the Panciatichi, but once again no vegetables were served; rather, the focus was on meats of various kinds as was fairly typical of medieval banquets. Everyone served sugared almonds, even Prudenzani's signore did. But where are the torte, such as a *Torta Parmigiana*? None of the meals outlined in the documents for either Panciatichi or Bandinelli note a torta with one exception: Bandinelli did serve "due gran torte di marcaponi" (a mascarpone torta), which were given as gifts and served at the very last banquet on Christmas Day.[13] At the first and last dinner, Panciatichi served tartare (also noted in the Prudenzani meals), a type of large, open-faced, custard torta without a crust; sixty of them had to be made.[14] Elaborate tortes like the *Torta Parmigiana* are not among the creations at Datini meals either, nor any of the meals outlined in Claudio Benporat's book on banquets from this period. Terrence Scully does discuss how popular the *Torta Parmigiana* was, though he cites only cookery books, not actual menus.[15] One banquet for the January 24, 1416, wedding in Florence of Antonio di Niccolo Castellani, for which we have no specific details, is a curious list of what needed to be purchased for several meals (including a fairly elaborate torta), what was need for each table, and the number of servers (sixteen). Like the Panciatichi and Bandenelli meals, meat dominated and tregea was served at every meal. The most extensive list was for the Tuesday morning meal, which included the ingredients needed to make sixty torte (pork, fresh cheese (giuncade), orange juice, grapes, crushed cloves, crushed pepper, fine spices, whole pine nuts, and saffron) and the ingredients for making ravioli; cheese and eggs were also listed, but they were probably a separate dish and not part of the torta. The question remains: who made and served such an elaborate dish? We'll return to this question at the end of this chapter.

Even the most astounding banquet menus were little more than very long lists of quite normal dishes. Grand banquets began with the same dishes as the cook prepared for any dinner and continued during the lengthy succession of courses by an accumulation of dishes that were served at a similar point in just about any regular meal. Great feasts cost money. The cook, in consequence, was expected to put on a splendid show while at the same time to trim expenses wherever a corner could be cut. Not everyone was served all the dishes. The most luxurious dishes were reserved for the most important people present. Even for those in the charmed circle of privilege, there were careful gradations in the actual amounts offered to each person. Rank had its own distinct advantage. Behind the scenes, the cook and all the other senior officers in the kitchen quarters had to keep a sharp eye out for what was to be saved and recycled, and they cut down on waste of every kind.[16]

Orchestrating and Serving the Meal

In the late Middle Ages, there was no such thing as a dining room or dining hall; no room was set aside as a place specifically or exclusively meant for eating. In a large household, the master, even when eating with his immediate family, might decide to take his meals in the intimacy of his own apartment, in the antecamera. However, usually, there was one room in the household spacious enough for relatively large public gatherings, a multi-functional room—the *sala* in Italy—that was also used for dining with guests. As we have seen in previous chapters, the Datini used the loggia off the downstairs kitchen for dining and also a room nearby the "room with two beds" for dining when guests were present. Generally the same as any room in the house, except it was larger, had a higher ceiling, and had a fireplace to warm the room; it might have a musician's loft. A stairway from a lower floor or a covered passageway from a separate wing connected the kitchen to dining area.[17]

Food itself, though essential to the plan, was only one element in the staging of the affair. Ceremonials and the rituals of service had their parts to play (Figure 5.1). Fine linens and handsome tableware lent their own luster to the scene. Dignity, decorum, and magnificence raised the tone. Dishes prepared in the kitchen had to be deemed worthy of the occasion when they were presented at the table.[18] No feast could begin until the cooks had done their work. The tables had to be laid, the diners seated, and the officers of the household with parts to play in the production had taken their places. There was a sense of occasion, of rising expectation, of a gathering wave about to crest. In this pause, the senior officer sent a messenger to the kitchen that they were ready for service. Only after the cook had received the signal to go ahead was his master informed that everything was in order and the show could be set in motion.[19] Borso d'Este's "apparechiadore" (table decorator) laid his table for dinner service, changed the tablecloths, plates, and napkins throughout the courses, and brought water so Borso could wash his hands, whereas Gatamelata, his *sescalco* (chief steward), served at his

Figure 5.1 Banquet, detail of Luttrell Psalter (1335–1340), MS 42130, fol. 166v. British Library, London, UK. Source: Commons.Wikimedia.org.

table cutting meat and attending to Borso's needs. Borso also had a *credenziero* (*credenza* steward), Marco Bruno.[20]

Those who attended a banquet were seated at their tables according to rank, often with women seated separately from men, as we saw at the 1388 morning meal hosted by Giovanni Panciachiti in Pistoia.[21] Tables were not a stationary piece of furniture as they are today, but had to be brought into wherever the meal was to take place and assembled at meal time along with folding chairs for the head table and benches, sometimes with high backs and a cushioned seat, for the guests. The middle table—referred to as the high or head table, sometimes atop a raised platform, was reserved for the host and guests of honor. Behind this table, a festive covering of cloth hung suspended to emphasize the standing of the honored guest and to protect against drafts. Other tables were arranged on either side to form a "U" shape; diners sat along the outer edge allowing service and the presentation of dishes, as well as entertainment, in the center. Each table was covered with a white tablecloth and a second cloth, displaced to the side of the table where the diners sat, with half of it covering their laps, was used to wipe fingers and mouths during the meal. Each place setting consisted of a spoon, which did not appear regularly until the fourteenth century, and a round or square of trencher bread, sometimes placed over a plate of wood or metal; the knife was an indispensable implement at the medieval meal. While the host might provide his guests, both women and men, with a knife, it was more common for guests to bring their own personal knives with them—their constant companion and invaluable possession, it functioned as both an eating tool and defensive weapon. For the host to offer his guests a knife from his own set of cutlery was often a gesture of honor.[22] To amaze his guests on special occasions, Francesco Datini brought out thirty-six silver forks in sheaths.[23] The forks were not a common eating utensil; rather, they were used for prying foods out of jars, cups, and the like instead of using one's fingers. Small finger bowls were set along the table and the water occasionally changed throughout the meal. Salt was set out on the tables in a variety of holders ranging from simple to ornate. At the head table, the host's most prized possession—a salt-boat or nef, a valuable work of silver, was a sign by which the guest could measure his or her status, according to the distance he or she was from the host's saltcellar. Two to four guests shared platters and bowls, finger bowls, and flagons, indicating a measure of friendship.[24]

Liquid refreshments were placed on a table (*credenza* or sideboard) against the wall and near the head table; it held pitchers, ewers, basins, bowls, platters, plates, saltcellars, and spice-candy dispensers—all of valuable materials like silver. The display was meant to reflect the opulence of the family. From here, the person in charge of beverage service carried out his duties. The carver, usually a gentleman of the upper classes, oversaw the carving of the meat at the high table. The art of carving was part of the schooling of a nobleman. At the surrounding tables, the guests themselves carved their own meat. After grace was said and hands washed from a bowl carried around by a servant with a towel, servants wearing the colors of their masters filed in carrying the dishes of the first course. The name of each dish was called out loud.[25] Those of higher standing received larger portions and better quality food. Only the most prominent guests were permitted to have their food served directly on their personal plates; elsewhere guests helped themselves from the same platter. While elsewhere in Europe, the common number of course was three, in Italy guests were served as many as eight to twelve courses. Each course included a number of different dishes brought to the table simultaneously. Each guest helped himself or herself to the dishes within easy reach—no passing of dishes as we do today.[26] Almost all the food was prepared so that it was easily picked up and eaten with either the fingers, the point of a knife, or a spoon.

At the beginning of a festive meal, sweet pastries, candied fruit, confectionaries, and sweet wines were served to stir the appetite. The first formal course consisted of soups and pies, and the meal ended with palate-cleansing jellies. Affluent medieval diners ate a wide assortment of birds: swan, capon, partridge, heron, cormorant, and wild duck. Baby animals and immature meats, such as veal, were favored over older, rougher meats, like beef, which ended up in the stockpot. Bread was an essential part of the meal. Bread trenchers were used to soak up juices; once the meal was over, they were either given to the poor or used as thickeners in stews, soups, and sauces. Ordinary people celebrated in a similar way, though their feasts were comprised of fewer courses and dishes, and the sweet starters, desserts, and digestives were lacking altogether. The poorest households served a single dish of food.[27] In contrast to the grand banquet or even the upper-class daily meal, in peasant cottages, warm food was brought to the table in the cooking pot and cold dishes were served in bowls or on wooden platters (see Figure 5.2). Diners helped themselves to the food with their fingers, though everyone kept a personal knife and spoon. In ordinary homes, people sat around the hearth to dine.[28]

The feast was the sum of many parts; its aim was to satisfy many senses, and the creations the cook sent to the table were judged in this context. The visual appeal of the food set on the table had to compete for applause with the drama of action and gesture in the ceremony of service. Carving at the high table was a spectator sport in which the way the carver handled his tools was appraised by knowledgeable, unkindly, critical eyes. The carver had to know how to carve every creature from heron to beaver, and how to cut delicate, bite-sized portions, laying them in precise patterns on a plate, spoon on the appropriate sauce, and finally, present the finished dish in the correct manner to his lord. He had to repeat the process for each of those deemed worthy to be honored with such attention. Carving was an art that demanded much skill. The drama of serving the meat was matched by the visual excitement

Figure 5.2 A Meal around a Fire, miniature from *Tacuunum Sanitatis*, fourteenth century, facsimile of the original, P. Pazzini, E. Pirani, and M. Salmi, eds., Rome: Franco Maria Ricci, 1970. Source: Photo courtesy of the author.

that grand goblets and handsome platters contributed to the occasion. To vie with such splendor, cooks sometimes added their own finishing touches of gold to a dish, using foil to trim a plate or a piecrust, or to highlight one feature by gilding the claw of a peacock or the beak of a swan. Strong color contrasts of reds, greens, blues, and yellows added visual excitement to any dish and bring to mind the reds and blues used in the contemporary paintings of Duccio and Giotto. The visual triumph of art over nature kindled the medieval imagination.[29]

Cooking and Eating with the Datini

We have already seen how complex it was for the Panciatichi household to organize a series of banquets to celebrate his nomination to *cavaliere*, even with an extensive staff. But what would you do if your husband asked you to host a prestigious cardinal who was in the neighborhood attending to the pope without having an exact date for his and his retinue's arrival? This is exactly what Francesco Datini asked of his wife Margherita in January 1410. Francesco escaped to Florence as he felt too ill to entertain such an eminent guest and instructed his wife to do so in his place. In early January 1410, Alexander's papal court was staying at Pistoia, not far from Prato, and several of the prelates and court dignitaries planned to visit the Datini at Prato.[30] Most of Margherita's attention was given to preparing for the arrival of the eminent French cleric and theologian, Pierre d'Ailly, bishop of Cambrai and bishop of Le Puy, whom the Datini called the cardinal of Pau. Francesco told Margherita, "act in such a way that I receive honor and that the cardinal receives honor from me," and Margherita responded, "Everything will be done in a way that brings them honor."[31] Of course, Margherita had hosted many elite guests in her home in Prato when Francesco was elsewhere (and we will come back to those events later), but this occasion was quite different. She did not know exactly when the guest would arrive or how many might come with him. She waited daily for word and wrote at least once if not twice a day to Francesco keeping him informed of the situation as he required her to do—he monitored her. Her letters to Francesco show her anxiety over the preparation for the event and over pleasing Francesco, who was ever critical of her.[32]

From the very start, Margherita's letters give us insight into just how complicated Francesco's request to host the cardinal was. On the morning of Wednesday, January 3, 1410, the cardinal was expected Saturday evening; by Wednesday afternoon, his emissary told Margherita it would be many days, but he would let her know in plenty of time. Margherita wrote to Francesco: "We will offer him and his retinue hospitality here in our house and . . . you will be informed about what follows. Regarding provisions . . . we have simply bought a calf for [ten] florins, which is still big enough for us to have plenty of food to do him honor should he come tomorrow or the next day. We have poultry and everything else prepared so that everything will go smoothly and in an orderly way. We arranged with the butcher to get another calf if we need it."[33] Then next day she was still waiting, telling Francesco that perhaps he would come in the next couple of days, but she began to worry about the veal. Fortunately, she had obtained chickens to kill later. By January 5, still waiting for word, she spent some time selecting the best of their red and white wines for the cardinal and lesser ones for his companions. On January 6, she wrote to Francesco: "So he [the cardinal] is keeping us in suspense and has still not sent us word. We have no idea when he is coming, which is bad news as far as the calf is concerned. Given the expense, we would not like giving it away to just anyone."[34] So she made a plan to distribute the meat to friends in Prato and Florence if the cardinal did not show up. But then a messenger came saying the cardinal might come the next day: "So we stopped, had the butcher examine it and he thought it would last until Thursday and would be even better than today."[35] In the midst of all this, Messer Giovanni Genovardi (on his way to see the cardinal) arrived at Cambio's Inn and Margherita tried to persuade him to come to her house. He said no, so she sent him "white wine from Lucca, some cheeses and some apples. He was very pleased. . . . Tomorrow he is leaving and we will try our best to give him a meal."[36] Genovardi reassured her that he would let her know when the cardinal was coming. The following day, Margherita decided to send some of the veal to Francesco in Florence and gave the rest away. Finally, on January 8, two of the cardinal's servants arrived in the evening to say the cardinal would be there the next morning (January 9), and Margherita informed Francesco: "We ordered the meat they wanted from the butcher. They will be given everything and we will pay for bread, wine, sweets and other things. We have everything ready to treat him with honor. We do not know how long he will stay. . . . The servants who came were amazed at such hospitality."[37]

Fortunately, the cardinal brought his own cook and Margherita supplied him with all the ingredients necessary to prepare all the meals for fifty people. Margherita wrote to Francesco that the cardinal did not need to spend money and that the cardinal was pleased. Imagine how nerve wracking it would be to wait day after day, yet having to be prepared for the cardinal's arrival at any moment. Think of the complexity of organizing every aspect of the event, except the actual cooking. Talk about meal planning! She worried about waste—the veal going bad—so she gave it away and had to buy more later on. Imagine the costs! She paid for everything—food for fifty people, grain, and hay and stalls for the horses, and she had to find places for people to sleep. While this may not have been an unusual situation for someone of her stature—to be on beck and call and to provide every possible thing—we have actual letters that tell us far more than documents recording events like those for the Panciatichi celebrations.

A few years earlier, Francesco Datini and Margherita hosted the wedding banquet for his daughter Ginevra on April 24, 1407, at their palazzo in Prato. It probably took place on the ground floor in the loggia or in the "room with two beds" that also was used for entertaining, rather than in the upstairs *sala*, which was rather small. The meal was likely prepared in the lower kitchen, which was larger than the upstairs one and within easy access to the loggia. Francesco hired a cook, Mato di Stincone, "cuoco" and paid him four florins and ten scudi for the single meal—a substantial amount if you consider that one of their maids earned ten florins a year. Six servants were also hired to assist Francesco's own staff to wait on the tables; they were given new tunics of scarlet cloth and hose.[38] Ginevra, Francesco's illegitimate daughter (adopted by Margherita and Francesco) by Lucia, their white slave, who was later freed and married, was to marry Lionardo di Tommaso di Giunta, a first cousin of Noccolo di Giunta, Francesco's friend and partner in the cloth trade. Ginevra was fourteen years old when the betrothal took place, and her father provided her with a dowry worth a thousand florins, more than many daughters of great Florentine merchants; it included 161 florins in cash and the rest in "donora" or gifts: fine clothing and fabric, furnishings and chests, etc.[39]

For the wedding, what was Margherita's role? Certainly, she would not sit idly by and watch, though she would have to defer to both Francesco and the cook. She certainly would have done some organization before the cook arrived. As we have already seen, Margherita knew how to plan for any event and would have had everything ready in the lower kitchen for the cook, perhaps gathering ingredients from the kitchen garden; making sure the verjuice and pork jelly (gelatin or aspic) were made; instructing household servants to clean the spits, pots, pans, and cooking utensils; taking care to have both water from the well and firewood brought in; and having enough good bread made. Francesco ordered the food: he bought 310 pounds of fish from the Bisenzio (a river) at the cost of fourteen florins and seven pounds of veal. They used thirty-one pounds of lard in preparing the meal, and it was likely house-made. The banquet consisted of three courses for fifty guests. They started with ravioli, tortellini (in a broth), and blancmange. The main course included veal, capon, fish (perhaps roasted and served with a sauce), and at least two pies, which were generally made with pork, chickens, ham, eggs, dates, almonds, flour, spices, saffron, sugar, and salt, not unlike our *Torta Parmigiana*, though without the ravioli inside.[40] Musicians played and comfits were passed around, after which the bride was taken in a wedding procession to her husband's home. Within a week, Ginevra was back at her parent's home for another banquet which cost a mere one florin and twelve soldi.[41] Just for the sake of comparison, it is of interest to note what Francesco purchased for his own wedding celebrations in 1377: 406 loaves of bread, 250 eggs, a hundred pounds of cheese, two quarters of an ox, sixteen quarters of mutton, thirty-seven capons, eleven chickens, two boar's heads, and feet for jelly and the wines came from Provence and Tuscany.[42] Unfortunately, we do not know how many attended or the menu for the banquet; clearly the emphasis was on meat. Curiously, though, there was no veal, his favorite.

Margherita often hosted illustrious guests on her own, but with very specific instructions from Francesco, whose honor was at stake. For example, on January 3, 1410, Francesco instructed Margherita to offer hospitality to Messer Marco from Venice, and she wrote to him: "Messer Marco dined and slept here last night . . . we received him in the best possible manner. He said it had been a long time since he had been treated so well."[43] Even earlier, in 1394, Margherita made sure that she was home to receive the sister of the eminent Florentine Messer Giovanni Panchiatichi (whom we met earlier in this chapter) and his sister's family. They spent the night at the palazzo: Margherita wrote, "Messer Giovanni Panciatichi's sister Monna Lionarda and her daughter Monna Sandra arrived at the [twenty-fourth] hour and the son of Monna Sandra was with them. They stayed the night and in the morning, they ate here. I tried to provide the best hospitality I could, but it was not possible to do this very well because all the fish smelled bad. . . . We did our best to serve them honorably with other food."[44]

One afternoon in June 1398, local and Florentine dignitaries, including the Podesta, came to view the Villa il Palco.[45] Margherita reported that she and Niccolo di Piero bought a lot of sweets (with the plan of keeping any leftover for themselves), oranges, and beautiful cherries. They provided white wine they had bought from a friend and some of their own white wine, as well as bread, napkins, and everything that was necessary. Niccolo di Piero, Barzalone, and other friends were there to converse with the guests, but Margherita did not attend. Margherita wrote of the event to Francesco:

> Ubaldo di Fatto sent me a message to say that he, the podesta, and all their people wanted to go to Il Palco this morning. So I sent Niccolo di Piero to enquire whether they were in fact going. Ubaldo replied that they had decided to, but that we should not send anything, because if they knew we were doing so, they would not go. Niccolo and I thought it right to buy some candied pine nuts and to give them what we had leftover. We took the box of sweets, and we sent a lot of oranges and beautiful cherries and some of the white wine you bought from Nanni, as well as our own house wine, and bread, napkins and everything else that was necessary. Niccolo, Barzalone, Benedetto, Bretone and Angelo have gone there. Nicolo also offered them the mules. They accepted and were very grateful because they had left their own mounts in Florence. Ubaldo, Arriguccio and our Nanni went with them.[46]

On another occasion when Margherita was to host the wife and daughter of Guido del Palagio at Prato, Francesco told her to serve "a roast of twelve capons and two kids . . . or roast pork and salad," as well as the pork jelly she had just made.[47] Surely Margherita would have served her guests other delicacies, as well as bread and wine. Guido himself came frequently to spend time with Francesco, his close friend, Prato. On August 25, 1392, for example, he came with his wife, the daughter of Giovanni Panciatichi, and a group of friends. To treat them with the respect that was due them, Francesco and Margherita served them a sumptuous lunch: fish worth five florins; rump, breast, and hind leg of veal; forty gelding hooves to make a gelatin; one hundred oranges at four denari each; sixteen and a half pounds of Pisa cheese to make a "mistico" served with vegetables, presumably raw; six pairs of rock pigeons; and a pair of ducks for Guido since he did not like pigeon.[48] Francesco's notebook only records what he ordered for the event, but nothing about the meal itself, how it was cooked, or the number of courses. Presumably, for this meal and the two that followed, no professional cook was hired; rather, it is likely that Margherita oversaw what went on in the kitchen.

For a dinner served on August 18, Francesco requested the following menu. The first course: zuccata (candied gourd) in white wine or with vermillion, and gelatin for "solcio" (shaped and marinated meat). The second course of roasts: two ducks, one loin of pork weighing six pounds (meats were bought daily and served with appetizing sauces), six pairs of chickens and six pairs of pigeons (perhaps their own); for fritters: milk for eight cheese (presumably, they made the cheese as we saw in chapter 4), three pairs of cheeses and sixteen to twenty oranges (perhaps from their own garden), and giuncade (fresh cheese) served on its own. Fruit to finish the meal included pears, fennel, and some peaches, and at the end of the meal treggea (sugared almonds) and white wine were served.[49] As well, it is likely the meal would have included vegetables from their own garden, their own bread, and their own wine for the other courses. Gelatin would have to be made, and Margherita knew how to do it, as we saw in chapter 4. How were the meats roasted? We wonder what sauce or sauces were used. How was the fruit served? What was Margherita's role here? Surely the meat was ordered well in advance of the meal as it was for the 1410 meal discussed earlier. This must have been a fairly small group and not unlike the meal Francesco planned for his homecoming (see the beginning of this chapter).

On another occasion, Francesco organized a dinner party for a diverse group of men (no women were invited) in terms of social status and background; it was held at Prato and several of the guests stayed until the morning.[50] Among others, the guest listed included Guido del Palagio and his nephew, Ser Lapo Mazzei, Francesco's notary and family friend, Giovanni di Gherardo, jurist and mathematician Turrigo Pugliesi, a Prato aristocrat, and Tommaso del Bianchi, friend of Francesco's from his Avignon days. The menu for the first evening meal included chicken and pigeons, ducks, gelatin, cheese (presumably eaten separately), and cheese, milk, eggs, lard, and sugar for fritters. For the morning, Francesco ordered veal and capons boiled with pumpkin, sugared fruit, and white wine. So once again we have more or less the same dishes served to these guests as at the previous meal. And no women were present!

While the Datini household ate well when Francesco was at home in Prato, Margherita tended to serve rather simple meals when she and her household were on their own—simple dishes like those peas we've discussed in previous chapters! Even when Francesco was present, the meals the servants received were quite different from what Francesco, Margherita, and their close relatives and business associates ate. Their meals were much more limited in terms of dishes compared to what we have just been discussing. For example, while the Datini and their intimates ate expensive fish dishes in abundance in the days before Easter, the servants ate small quantities of much cheaper salted anchovies with a few herbs. The meals provided for the laundry women were equally frugal, consisting of low-quality cheese and pork liver, whereas the men working on repairs of the house received snacks of fava beans. This of course was not unusual in the Middle Ages when diet was based on social status.[51] However, everyone in the household received both bread and wine, though the servants were served a lower quality of each. In times of illness, the servants and staff were fed quite well to aid their recovery, and sometimes there were special meals. In November 1384, for example, Francesco decided to gather his employees together at Prato for a meal that included boiled hares with pappardelle, roast chicken, and pears cooked in spiced wine. He served them Greco wine with "bericoccoli" (similar to ricciarelli biscuits, which are made of almonds).[52]

The Datini have served in this chapter and throughout the book as an example of a "real-life" family as opposed to more theoretical works such as the cookery books; they are the thread that runs through this book. In this chapter, the letters between Francesco and Margherita tell us in some detail just how complex and frustrating planning meals for guests could be. Their letters serve as a counterbalance to documents like those for the Panciatichi and Bandinelli events and even the imaginary meals of Sermini and Prudenzani. Throughout this chapter, we have noted what was commonly served at nearly every one of the meals here—the sugared almonds, for example. Yet we have noted, too, that some dishes are missing. Our *Torta Parmingiano*, for example, seems only to be found in cookery books and not on actual menus, and we wonder why that is. Was it meant to dazzle or impress the reader of the book? It makes one wonder if such marvels were ever made and how useful for cooking all these cookery books were! Perhaps such dishes were made for the noble and elite, though even looking at the five menus in *Cuoco Napoletano*, which is at the very end of our period and beyond the scope of this book, there are only simple torte: "torta inglese," "torta Bianca," and "torta with herbs and peas"—one menu was for an elaborate banquet for the archbishop of Benevento and another for the ordination of Monsignore Ascanio Sforza as prince of Capua. He was the brother of Ludovico, il Moro, duke of Milan and Bari.[53] Incidentally, a recipe for the *Torta Parmigiana* is not included in this recipe collection.

A Few Last Words

This has been the story of the medieval kitchen and its operation during the heyday of Middle Ages. We have explored the kitchen from its location and layout looking at Francesco Datini's palazzo in Prato as an example of a "real" kitchen, to its equipment: the hearth, the fuels, the vessels and implements, and how they were used to prepare a meal. We considered who actually did the cooking and who assisted them, looking at how the kitchen was staffed and who did what. As well, we surveyed the variety of ingredients available to the cook: spices, herbs, meats, fruits, and vegetables. We discussed food preservation and production: salted fish, cured meats, and cheesemaking, for example. To gain a clear picture of the medieval kitchen and its operation, we turned to cookery books, gastronomic texts, household inventories, letters, and literary sources. We ended our journey in the mid-fifteenth century at the time of Maestro Martino of Como, whose cookery book paved the way to a new era, the Renaissance.[54]

Just what about Martino's work marks the shift from the Middle Ages to the Renaissance? Martino changed the way people ate; he employed spices and other ingredients to enhance food rather than disguise it, and he downplayed the use of hot, Eastern spices and made use instead of herbs from his own garden such as parsley, celery, and onions.[55] He also elevated vegetables to a new level; small game birds replaced large haunches of roast meats. His recipes in his treatise-like compendium reveal the secrets and tricks of the trade. Moreover, the recipes are divided into chapters according to the types of food (meats, broths, soups, pastas, sauces and seasonings, tortes, eggs and omelets, and fish), and he gave the number of people the recipe would serve, the quantities and kinds of ingredients required, the proper method of cooking, the most suitable cookware to achieve the desired results, and the time required to cook a dish—quite the opposite of what we discovered while exploring our medieval cookery books. Eating methods changed: the fork replaced the knife for spearing meat and then eating it, and trenchers, plates, communal bowls, and serving platters gave way to individual place settings. With the Renaissance, then, came the development of civilized manners.

Another significant change to note: unlike the Middle Ages where the cookery books were penned by anonymous cooks (with the exception of Johannes Bockenheim), with the Renaissance we know exactly who wrote the books: Maestro Martino of Como, Cristoforo da Messisbugo, and Bartolomeo Scappi are primary examples and, of course, through their book dedications we know who they work for and their audience.[56] The overall layout and equipment of the kitchen did not change dramatically, though as the centuries progress we see a change from primarily hearth cooking to the use of freestanding stoves and other equipment.[57] With the discovery of the New World, new foods were introduced into Italy, for example, turkey and tomatoes. The centuries that follow those covered in this book and moving beyond the early Renaissance mark many dramatic changes especially as we move into the seventeenth and eighteenth centuries, but that is another story altogether.

APPENDIX I

Note: I have intentionally followed the original Italian text as closely as possible rather than modernizing the recipe for comparison purposes within the chapters where it is discussed.

The Anonymous Tuscan's Torta Parmigiana[1]

Take chickens, dismember them, cut them up and fry them with finely chopped onions in the highest-quality pork fat. When the chicken has cooked awhile, add abundant spices and salt. Then take aromatic herbs with saffron of the highest quality and finely chop them. Next take the chicken from the fat and with a knife pulverize it into a paste. And mix it with the herbs and a quantity of grated cheese. Then take some of this mixture (setting some aside) and make ravioli. Next take some fresh cheese and make white ravioli. Also take parsley and other aromatic herbs and fresh cheese and make green ravioli and all these above said things, mix with egg. Also take whole almonds and pound them into a fine paste and divide them into two parts: one part, mix with spices of the best quality and the other, mix with sugar. And of the one and of the other make separate ravioli. Next take egg and stuff them. Take pork intestines well washed and stuff them with good herbs and cheese and boil them well. Take prosciutto crudo and slice it thinly to make a similar sausage. Then beat an egg and mix it with said chicken in a pot and brace it. Stir it with a ladle often. Take it off the fire and season with salt. Next take good flour and make a crust and form it into the manner of a baking dish or frying pan. Next with a spoon take the broth from the chicken and baste the crust. Then in this crust place a layer of meat from the chicken, then a layer of white ravioli with "savore" over it, then add another layer of prosciutto and sausage, cut up. The fourth layer, meat, next a layer of sausage made from pork intestine; the sixth layer, almond ravioli with a layer of dates and over this "il savore"; next, sprinkle with abundant spices so that it is covered. Brace it and put on the lid, "il testo." Open it often and smear with pork fat and close it. Take a fine crust and bathe it in water, break it, and put the hot "testo" over it.

APPENDIX II

Note: I have intentionally followed the original Italian text as closely as possible rather than modernizing the recipe for comparison purposes within the chapters where it is discussed.

The Anonymous Venetian's
Good Torta Parmigiana[1]

Torta Parmigiana for twenty-five people: Take eight "libre" of pork and take twelve fresh cheeses and take six aged cheeses and twenty-four eggs and half a "libre" of sweet spices and six chickens and four capons and take the pork and boil it well and when it is cooked mix it with a quantity of mint and parsley; and take six fresh cheeses and twenty-three eggs and enough salt pork fat and beat it with the spices and saffron. With these things make a good pesto ("battuto") and a good "zallo." Take two fresh cheeses and egg whites and mix and make nine white ravioli with "croste de pasta" and take two fresh cheeses and one aged cheese, mint and parsley and beat together and make twelve green ravioli. Take four cheeses and cut into thin slices to cover them. Take the chickens and dismember them and from each part, cut into two pieces. Fry them in salt pork fat and "strutto." Add spices and fry. Again, take one libre of pitted and skinned dates, cinnamon, ginger, cloves, and put these ravioli in boiling water. When they are done, pulverize sweet spices and put them inside with a crust over. This torta should be yellow and covered with pork fat and heavy with spices. You can make it for fewer or for more people. If you make it in a copper "testo," you will want a small fire; in a terracotta "testo," the same.

NOTES

Chapter 1

1. Terrence Scully, *The Art of Cookery in the Middle Ages* (Woodbridge, UK: Boydell Press, 1995), 3.

2. Anonimo Angevin, *Liber de coquina* in Emilio Faccioli, *L' arte della cucina in Italia, libri di recette e trattati sulla civilita della tavola dal XIV al XIX secolo* (Turin: Giulio Einuadi, Editore, 1987, 1992), 20–41; Anonimo Veneziano, *Libro per cuoco,* edited by Ludovico Frati (Bologna: Forni Editore, 1970, reprint of 1899 Liverno edition); Anonimo Toscano, *Libro della cucina*, edited by Francesco Zambrini (Bologna: Gaetano Romagnoli, 1863); Anonimo Medidonale, *Due libri di cucina*, edited by Ingmar Bostrom (Stockholm, Sweden: Almquist and Wiksell International, 1985); Terrence Scully, ed. *Cuoco Napolitano, the Neapolitan Recipe Collection, a Critical Edition and English Translation* (Ann Arbor: The Unversity of Michigan Press, 2000); Magninus Mediolanensis (Maino de' Maineri), *Opusculum de saporibus*, for a printed edition, see Terrence Scully, "Opusculum de Saporum of Magnius Mediolanensis," *Medium Aevium* 54 (1985): 175–207; Lynn Thorndike, "A Medieval Sauce Book," *Speculum*, 9/2 (April 1934): 183–90; Salomone Morpugo, ed. *LVII Recette d' un Libro di cucina del buon secolo della lingua*, (Bologna: Nicola Zanichelli, 1890; Olindo Guerini, ed. *Framento di un libro di cucina del secolo XIV* (Bologna: Nicola Zanichelli, 1887); Claudio Benporat, "La cucina dei 12 Ghiotti," *Appunti di gastronomia*, XXII (1997): 5–22 and his "Un ricettario di cucina trecentesco: ms 158/1 della Biblioteca Universitaria di Bologna," *Appunti di gastronomia*, LXII (2010): 5–30; Johannes Bockenheim, *Il registro di cucina di Papa Martino V*, edited by Giovanna Bonardi (Milan: Mondadori, 1995); Maestro Martino's *Il Libro de arte coquinaria* and Bartolomeo Sacchi, called Platina's *On Right Pleasure and Good Health.*

3. Ken Albala, *The Banquet, Dining in the Great Courts of Late Renaissance Europe* (Urbana & Chicago: University of Illinois Press, 2007), x.

4. Massimo Montanari, *Mediveal Tastes, Food, Cooking and the Table* (New York: Columbia University Press, 2015), 21; Gentile Sermini, *Novelle*, 2 vols, edited by Giuseppe Vettori (Perugia: Stab. Tip Grafica, 1968; Rome: A.T.E, 1968), Novella 29, 483–96.

5. Scully, *The Art of Cookery*, 7–8.

6. See note #2.

7. Bockenheim, *Il registro di cucina*.

8. Montanari, *Medieval Tastes*, 151.

9. Ibid, 152.

10. Bockenheim, *Il registro di cucina*, #42, #55.

11. Montanari, *Medieval Tastes*, 35–36.

12. Hannele Klemetila, *Medieval Kitchen: A Social History with Recipes* (London: Reakton Books, 2002), 73.

13. Scully, "Opusculum de Saporum of Magnius Mediolanensis," 175–207; Thorndike, "The Medieval Sauce Book," 183–90.

14. Scully, *The Art of Cookery*, 207.

15. Anonimo Veneziano, *Libro per cuoco*, #CXI; Faccioli, *L' arte della cucina in Italia*, 90.

16. Faccioli, *L' arte della cucina in Italia*, 48.

17. Montanari, *Medieval Tastes*, 21

18. Anonimo Veneziano, *Libro per cuoco*, 57–59, #CXII; Anonimo Toscano, *Libro della cucina*, 59–61. Other versions include Anonimo Meridionale's complex version written in Latin (Faccioli, *L'arte della cucina in Italia*, 103, #1 and 104), which is quite similar to Anonimo Toscano's, whereas *LVII Ricette* is almost identical to Anonimo Veneziano's recipe (Nicola Zanchelli, ed. p. 3, intro, refers to book as *Libro del Cuoco di Nicolo*).

19. The only other extant book from this period with a similar title is the *Libro del cuoco di Nicolo*, a fragment edited by Nicola Zanchelli. Both in Morpugo, ed. *LVII Recette d' un Libro di cucina del buon secolo della lingua* and in Guerini, ed. *Framento di un libro di cucina del secolo XIV*, the writer uses this phrasing "se vuoli fare una torta, togli."

20. Faccioli, *L'arte della cucina in Italia*, 80, #XIV.

21. Anne Willan, *The Cookbook Library* (Berkeley, Los Angeles, and London: University of California Press, 2012), 8–9.

22. Anne Crabb, *The Merchant of Prato's Wife: Margherita Datini and her World, 1360-1423* (Ann Arbor: University of Michigan Press, 2015), 78.

23. Carolyn James and Antonio Pagliaro, eds and trans. *Margherita Datini: Letters to Francesco Datini* (Toronto: Iter & Centre for Reformation & Renaissance Studies, The Other Voice Series, 2012), 201, #112, 21 March 1397.

24. See #4 and #32, #34, and #35.

25. The preservation of the Datini documents including account books, etc., was likely the result of Francesco's request in his will to create a "Ceppo"—a charity foundation for the poor housed in the Palazzo Datini at his death, ASPo, Fondo Ceppo.

26. The complex included a stable, his warehouse with office, and across the street an enclosed garden with fruit trees, a loggia and other buildings, a bake house, and a wine press. The house was expanded after he bought further property in 1405. Once this house was well underway, Francesco began to build a villa at Il Palco, his farm.

27. Archivio di Stato, Prato (hereafter: ASPo), Datini, Firenze-Prato, Francesco Datini, September 13, 1389.

28. Iris Origo, *The Merchant of Prato, Francesco di Marco Datini* (New York: Alfred Knopf, 1955), 203, "Mato di Stincone, cuoco."

29. Origo, *The Merchant of Prato*, 317.

30. Ibid, 317, 323.

31. Ibid, 317; James and Pagliaro, *Margherita Datini*, 116, #49, April 1, 1394; 227, #131, May 23, 1397.

32. Origo *The Merchant of Prato*, 318.

33. Ibid, 319.

34. Maria Luisa Incontri Lotteringhi della Stufa, *Pranzi e conviti, la cucina Toscana dal XVI secolo ai giorni d'oggi* (Florence: Edizioni Polistampa, 2010), 112–13.

35. Incontri Lotteringhi della Stufa, *Pranzi e conviti*, 212—and he wrote others: Un piatto di fagiuoli, Dell' aringa, Del Salsiccuolo, Di fave arrostite, radire e finnocchio, De pane e pecorino—Lorenzo de' Medici, *Poesie* (Florence: Barbera e Bianchi, 1859), 434, 435, 238, 294, 278.

36. Simone Prudenzani, *Il Saporetto con altri rime*, edited by Santore Debenedetti (Turin: Casa Editore, 1913), 123, #LIX (59).

37. Giovanni Sercambi, *Novelle*, edited by Giovanni Sinicropi (Bari: Gius, Laterza & Figli, 1972), vol. 2, 546, #123; Franco Sacchetti, *Il Trecento Novelle*, edited by Antonio Lanza (Florence: Sansoni Editore, 1984), 69, #XXXIV and 251, #CXXIV. As well, both fourteenth-century writers Giovanni Boccaccio in his *Decameron* and Dante Alighieri in his *Divine Comedy* frequently include tidbits about food and eating.

Chapter 2

1. Bridget Ann Henisch, *The Medieval Cook* (Woodbridge, UK: Boydell Press, 2009), 9.

2. Iris Origo, *The Merchant of Prato, Francesco di Marco Datini* (New York: Alfred Knopf, 1955), 3.

3. Luigi Alberto Gandini, *Tavola, cantina e cucina della Corte di Ferrara nel Quattrocento* (Modena: Societa Tipografica modenese, 1889), 51.

4. Allen Grieco, "Conviviality in the Renaissance Court: the 'Ordine et officij' and the Court of Urbino," in *Ordine et officif de casadi lo illustrissimo signor duca de Urbino*, edited by Sabine Eiche (Urbino: Accademia Raffaello, 1999), 41–44.

5. Terrence Scully, *The Art of Cookery in the Middle Ages* (Woodbridge, UK: Boydell Press, 1995), 241.

6. Gandini, *Tavola, cantina e cucina*, 51.

7. Anne Willan, *The Cookbook Library* (Berkeley, Los Angeles and London: University of California Press, 2012), 59.

8. Scully, *The Art of Cookery*, 241, 243.

9. Platina (Bartolomeo Sacchi), *Platina: On Right Pleasure and Good Health: A Critical Edition and Translation of De honesta voluptate et valetudine*, edited and translated by Mary Ella Milham (Tempe, AZ: Medieval and Renaissance Texts and Studies, 1998), I, 119.

10. Scully, *The Art of Cookery*, 253.

11. Willan, *The Cookbook Library*, 59.

12. Alberto Capatti and Massimo Montanari, *Italian Cuisine, a Cultural History* (New York: Columbia University Press, 1999), 218.

13. Henisch, *Medieval Cook*, 17, 19, 115, 127, 140.

14. Scully, *The Art of Cookery*, 239–40.

15. Terrence Scully, ed. *Cuoco Napolitano, the Neapolitan Recipe Collection, a Critical Edition and English Translation* (Ann Arbor: The Unversity of Michigan Press, 2000), 33.

16. Capatta and Monanari, *Italian Cuisine*, 216–17; Hannele Klemetila, *Medieval Kitchen: A Social History with Recipes* (London: Reakton Books, 2002), 17; Scully, *The Art of Cookery*, 87, 243–44, 251.

17. Grazia Rossanigo and Pier Luigi Muggrati, *Amandole e malvasia per uso di corte, cibi e ricette per la tavola dei Duchi di Milano* (Milan: Editore Aesthesis, 1998), 10.

18. Grieco, "Conviviality in the Renaissance Court," in *Ordine et officif*, 41–44.

19. Brown, R. V., *Enrique de Villena's "Arte Asoria," a Critical Edition and Study*, PhD dissertation, University of Wisconsin, 1974.

20. Claudio Benporat, *Feste e banchetti: convivialita italiana fra Tre e Quattrocento* (Florence: Leo S. Olschki, Editore, 2001), 27, 37–38.

21. Anonimo Toscano, *Libro della cucina*, edited by Francesco Zambrini (Bologna: Gaetano Romagnoli, 1863), 59–61.

22. Klemitila, *Medieval Kitchen*, 17.

23. Iris Origo, *The Merchant of Prato, Francesco di Marco Datini* (New York: Alfred Knopf, 1955), 183, Francesco to Margherita, May 7, 1394.

24. Origo, *The Merchant of Prato*, 207; Anne Crabb, *The Merchant of Prato's Wife: Margherita Datini and her World, 1360–1423* (Ann Arbor: University of Michigan Press, 2015), 101.

25. Crabb, *The Merchant of Prato's Wife*, 81–82, 84.

26. Origo, *The Merchant of Prato*, 179, 189, Francesco's letters to Margherita, dated April 8, 1394, April 11, 1398, May 23, 1397, and July 13, 1398.

27. Crabb, *The Merchant of Prato's Wife*, 66, 69.

28. Carolyn James and Antonio Pagliaro, eds. and trans. *Margherita Datini: Letters to Francesco Datini* (Toronto: Iter & Centre for Reformation & Renaissance Studies, The Other Voice Series, 2012), 318, #194, December 5, 1398.

29. Ibid, 282–83, #175, August 22, 1398.

30. Ibid, 201, #112.

31. Ibid, 190, #104, September 1, 1395.

32. Archivio di Stato, Prato, Inventario di Prato, Aprile 1399, Datini, 236/8, cc 51–54, published in Jerome Hayez and Diana Toccafondi, eds, *Palazzo Datini a Prato, una casa fatta per durare mille anni* (Florence: Edizione Polistampa, 2012), vol. II, 587–94; see Crabb, *The Merchant of Prato's Wife*, 95–96, 213.

33. James and Pagliaro, *Margherita Datini*, 207, #115, May 30, 1397; 211, #217, April 1, 1397; 325, #200, February 23, 1399; 335, #208, April 25, 1399.

34. Ibid, 144, #49, April 1, 1394.

Chapter 3

1. *Ordine et officif de casa di lo illustrissimo signor duca de Urbino*, edited by Sabine Eiche (Urbino: Accademia Raffaello, 1999), chapter 35, 118–19.

2. Anonimo Veneziano, *Libro per cuoco*, ed. Ludovico Frati (Bologna: Forni Editore, 1970, reprint of 1899 Liverno edition); Anonimo Toscano, *Libro della cucina*, edited by Francesco Zambrini (Bologna: Gaetano Romagnoli, 1863); Johannes Bockenheim, *Il registro di cucina di Papa Martino V*, edited by Giovanna Bonardi (Milan: Mondadori, 1995).

3. Terrence Scully, *The Art of Cookery in the Middle Ages* (Woodbridge, UK: Boydell Press, 1995), 86–88, 93; Anne Willan, *The Cookbook Library* (Berkeley: University of California Press, 2012), 58.

4. Franco Sacchetti, *Il Trecento Novelle*, edited by Antonio Lanza (Florence: Sansoni Editore, 1984), 70, #XXXIV.

5. Scully, *The Art of Cookery*, 96.

6. Ibid, 93.

7. Barbara Santich, *The Original Mediterranean Cuisine: Medieval Recipes for Today* (Chicago: Chicago Press Review, 1995), 45; Scully, *The Art of Cookery*, 93.

8. Dale Kent, "'The Lodging House of Memories,' an accountant's home in Renaissance Florence," *Journal of the Society of Architectural Historians* 66/4 (December 2007): 451–54.

9. Scully, *The Art of Cookery*, 88.

10. Ibid, 95–96.

11. Santich, *The Original Mediterranean Cuisine*, 16.

12. Sacchetti, *Il Trecento Novelle*, 250, #CXXIV.

13. Inventario di Prato, Octobre 1394, Archivio di Stato, Prato (hereafter, ASPo), Datini, 215/1; Inventario di Prato, Settembre 1405, ASPo, Datini 236/8, cc. 73–74 published in Jerome Hayez and Diana Toccafondi, eds, *Palazzo Datini a Prato, una casa fatta per durare mille anni* (Florence: Edizione Polistampa, 2012), vol II, 581–87, 594–98; Simonetta Cavaciochi, "The Merchant and Building" in Giampietro Nigro, ed. *Francesco di Marco Datini: The Man, Merchant* (Florence: Florence University Press, 2010), 152.

14. Carolyn James and Antonio Pagliaro, eds. and trans. *Margherita Datini: Letters to Francesco Datini* (Toronto: Iter & Centre for Reformation & Renaissance Studies, The Other Voice Series, 2012), 201, #112.

15. Ibid, June 6, 1397, 230, #135; Maria Giagnascovo, "What Francesco and his Family Ate," in Giampietro Nigro, ed. *Francesco di Marco Datini*, 109.

16. Ibid, April 5, 1397, 214–15, #121.

17. Iris Origo, *The Merchant of Prato, Francesco di Marco Datini* (New York: Alfred Knopf, 1955), 317, the letter dates October 15, 1397.

18. James and Pagliaro, *Margherita Datini*, Octover 25, 1397, 241, #144; Chiara Marcheschi, "'In Prato chon 24 bocche in chasa,' le donne della 'famgglia domestica' di Francesco e Margherita Datini" in Hayez and Toccafondi, ed. *Palazzo Datini a Prato*, vol. I, 210.

19. Emilio Faccioli, *L'arte della cucina in Italia, libri di recette e trattati sulla civilita della tavola dal XIV al XIX secolo* (Turin: Giulio Einuadi, Editore, 1987, 1992), 59; see also Johannes Bockenheim, *Il registro di cucina di Papa Martino V*, 7, #3.

20. Inventario di Prato, Aprile 1399, ASPo, Datini, 236/8, cc 51–54 published in Hayez and Toccafondi, ed. *Palazzo Datini a Prato*, vol. II, 587–94.

21. Faccioli, *L'arte della cucina in Italia*, 58.

22. Ibid, 59.

23. Inventario di Prato, Aprile 1399, ASPo, Datini, 236/8, cc 51–54 published in Hayez and Toccafondi, ed. *Palazzo Datini a Prato*, vol. II, 587–94.

24. Franco Sacchetti, *Il Trecento Novelle*, edited by Antonio Lanza (Florence: Sansoni Editore, 1984) and Gentile Sermini, *Novelle*, 2 vols, edited by Giuseppe Vettori (Perugia: Stab. Tip Grafica, 1968; Rome: A.T.E, 1968).

25. Hannele Klemettila, *The Medieval Kitchen, a Social History with Recipes* (London: Reaktion Books, 2012), 60–61; Willan, *The Cookbook Library*, 58; Scully, *The Art of Cookery*, 94–95.

26. Faccioli, *L'arte della cucina in Italia*, 91.

27. Ibid, 61.

28. Ibid, 23, #1, 6.

29. Ibid, 52, 83.

30. Ibid, 55.

31. Gentile Sermini, *Novelle*, 489, #29.

32. Anonimo Veneziano, *Libro per cuoco*; Anonimo Toscano, *Libro della cucina*; Faccioli *L'arte della cucina in Italia.*

33. Faccioli, *L'arte della cucina in Italia*, 29, #23, 59–60.

34. Inventario di Prato, Aprile 1399, ASPo, Datini, 236/8, cc 51–54 published in Hayez and Toccafondi, ed. *Palazzo Datini a Prato*, vol. II, 587–94.

35. Klemettila, *Medieval Kitchen*, 12, 19–20.

36. Brenda Preyer, "La struttura dell'abitare," in Hayez and Toccafondi, ed. *Palazzo Datini a Prato*, vol. I, 84–85.

37. For details about the Datini and the building of the palazzo, see chapter 1.

38. Philippe Bernardini, "Da un idea di 'paradiso' al Palazzo," in Hayez and Toccafondi, ed. *Palazzo Datini a Prato*, vol. I, 54, 55.

39. Preyer, "La struttura dell'abitare," in Hayez and Toccafondi, ed. *Palazzo Datini a Prato*, vol. I, 83.

40. Jerome Hayez, "Il migrante e il padrone, il palazzo nella vita di Francesco Datini," in Hayez and Toccafondi, ed. *Palazzo Datini a Prato*, vol. 1, 190, note #202 for the documents with names of guests.

41. Ibid, 188.

42. Claudio Cerritelli, "Il bel palagio, oroglio di Francesco," in Hayez and Toccafondi, ed. *Palazzo Datini a Prato*, vol. I, 27, 48.

43. Origo, *The Merchant of Prato*, 317, 321, 203; the 1399 inventory lists more: Inventario di Prato, Aprile 1399, ASPo, Datini, 236/8, cc 51–54 published in Hayez and Toccafondi, ed. *Palazzo Datini a Prato*, vol. II, 587–94.

44. Cavaciochi, "The Merchant and Building," 149.

45. James and Pagliaro, *Margherita Datini*, 115, #49, April 1, 1394; 137–38, #66, May 11, 1394.

46. Cavaciocchi, "The Merchant and Building," 148–49.

47. Ibid, 148–52.

48. Ibid, 132.

49. 1399 inventory of upstairs kitchen notes "abevercatoio da pipioni" (a watering pool), "3 stanghe dove dormono I polli" (perches): Inventario di Prato, Aprile

1399, ASPo, Datini, 236/8, cc 51–54 published in Hayez and Toccafondi, ed. *Palazzo Datini a Prato*, vol. II, 587–94.

50. James and Pagliaro, *Margherita Datini*, March 21, 1397, #112.

51. Cerritelli, "Il bel palagio, oroglio di Francesco," vol. I, 23.

52. Inventario di Prato, Aprile 1399, ASPo, Datini, 236/8, cc 51–54 published in Hayez and Toccafondi, ed. *Palazzo Datini a Prato*, vol. II, 591, 592.

53. Ibid, 583, 591.

54. Ibid, 591–99. In Iris Origo's monumental book, she suggests that both kitchens were sparsely furnished; however, the 1399 inventory suggests otherwise.

55. Ibid, 587–89.

56. Simonetta Cavaciocchi, "A Taste for Living," in Giampietro Nigro, ed. *Francesco di Marco Datini*, 205, APPo, Datini 236, cc 29, 30v, 57, and Datini, 615, c 262v.

57. Marco Spallanzani, "Lusterware of Valencia," in Giampietro Nigro, ed. *Francesco di Marco Datini*, 389–90.

58. Elena Cecchi, ed., *Le lettere di Francesco Datini alla moglie, Margherita (1385-1410)* (Prato: Societa Pratese di Storia Patria, 1990), January 20, 1395; for her response see, James and Pagliaro, *Margherita Datini*, January 21, 1395, 159, #82; Gragnasco, "What Francesco and his Family Ate," 106.

59. Cecchi, *Le lettere di Francesco Datini*, April 9, 1395, #63,132; Origo, *The Merchant of Prato*, 320.

60. James and Pagliaro, *Margherita Datini*, August 13, 1395, letter #101, 186–87.

61. Inventario di Prato, Aprile 1399, ASPo, Datini, 236/8, cc 51–54 published in Hayez and Toccafondi, ed. *Palazzo Datini a Prato*, vol. II, 591.

62. Ibid, 587.

63. Cavaciocchi, "The Merchant and Building," 154–55.

64. Inventario Post-Mortem di Ptrato, Agosto 1410, ASPo, Ceppi, 1618, cc 35–56 published in Hayez and Toccafondi, ed. *Palazzo Datini a Prato*, vol. II, 610.

Chapter 4

1. Anonimo Veneziano, *Libro per cuoco*, edited by Ludovico Frati (Bologna: Forni Editore, 1970, reprint of 1899 Liverno edition); Anonimo Toscano, *Libro della cucina*, edited by Francesco Zambrini (Bologna: Gaetano Romagnoli, 1863).

2. Simone Prudenzani, *Il Saporetto con altri rime*, edited by Santore Debenedetti (Turin: Casa Editore, 1913).

3. Anonimo Angevin, *Liber de coquina* in Emilio Faccioli, *L'arte della cucina in Italia, libri di recette e trattati sulla civiltà della tavola dal XIV al XIX secolo*

(Turin: Giulio Einuadi, Editore, 1987, 1992), 20–41; and Anonimo Veneziano, *Libro per cuoco*.

4. Terrence Scully, *The Art of Cookery in the Middle Ages* (Woodbridge, UK: Boydell Press, 1995), 6–8, 28–30.

5. Bridget Ann Henisch, *The Medieval Cook* (Woodbridge, UK: Boydell Press, 2009), 123–24.

6. Anonimo Toscano, *Libro della cucina*.

7. Magninus Mediolanensis (Maino de' Maineri), *Opusculum de saporibus*, for a printed edition, see Terrence Scully, "Opusculum de Saporum of Magnius Mediolanensis," *Medium Aevium* 54 (1985): 175–207, part III, chapters 10–21 of the book. See also Lynn Thorndike, "A Medieval Sauce Book," *Speculum*, 9/2 (April 1934): 183–90.

8. Simone Prudenzani, *Il Saporetto*, 102, #20, 123, #59.

9. Antonio Pucci, in Maria Luisa Incontri Lotteringhi della Stufa, *Pranzi e conviti, la cucina Toscana dal XVI secolo ai giorni d' oggi* (Florence: Edizioni Polistampa, 2010), 112–13.

10. This is not meant as a comprehensive list, but as an example of what was readily available.

11. Hannele Klemetila, *Medieval Kitchen: A Social History with Recipes* (London: Reakton Books, 2002), 52; Scully, *Art of Cookery*, 30.

12. Scully, *Art of Cooking*, 30, 31.

13. Ibid, 20–21; and Allan Evans, ed. *Francesco Balducci Pegolotti. La Practica della Mercatura* (Cambridge, MA: The Medical Academy of America, 1936), 21–315.

14. Alberto Capatti and Massimo Montanari, *Italian Cuisine, a Cultural History* (New York: Columbia University Press, 2003), 96.

15. Anonimo Veneziano, *Libro per Cuoco*, 37.

16. Scully, *Art of Cookery*, 52–53, 57.

17. Klemitilla, *The Medieval Kitchen*, 53, 55.

18. Faccioli, *L'arte della cucina in Italia*, 23–25, 47–52.

19. Anonimo Veneziano, *Libro per Cuoco*, 50, #XCV.

20. Scully, *Art of Cookery*, 70; Klemitilla, *The Medieval Kitchen*, 24, 25.

21. Ibid, 21; and Evans, ed. *Francesco Balducci Pegolotti*.

22. Archivio di Stato, Prato, Prato-Pisa, Francesco Datini, February 20, 1392.

23. Scully, *Art of Cookery*, 21; and Evans, ed. *Francesco Balducci Pegolotti*.

24. Olindo Guerini, ed. *Framento di un libro di cucina del secolo XIV* (Bologna: Nicola Zanichelli, 1887), 20, #5; and Claudio Benporat, "Un ricettario di cucina trecentesco: ms 158/1 della Biblioteca Universitaria di Bologna," *Appunti di gastronomia*, LXII (2010): 13, #5. Anonimo Toscano, *Libro della cucina*, 49, 55; Anonimo Veneneziano, *Libro per cuoco*, 49–50; Anonimo Angevin, *Liber de coquina* in Faccioli, *L'arte della cucina in Italia*, 37–39, #s 8, 9, 12, 13.

25. Terrence Scully, ed. *Cuoco Napolitano, the Neapolitan Recipe Collection, a Critical Edition and English Translation* (Ann Arbor: University of Michigan Press, 2000), 223. When lardo is salted or pickled, it is called "carne salata."

26. Anonimo Toscano, *Libro della cucina*, 57–58.

27. Ibid, "A fare agresto," 77.

28. Massimo Montanari, *Medieval Tastes, Food, Cooking and the Table* (New York: Columbia University Press, 2015), 111.

29. Ibid, 81, 85–86.

30. For the recipes see Faccioli, *L'arte della cucina in Italia*, 57, 59.

31. For the recipes see Faccioli, *L'arte della cucina in Italia*, 60, 61.

32. "Cascio Arrostito," Faccioli, *L'arte della cucina in Italia*, 66.

33. Archivio di Stato, Prato, Datini, Prato-Firenze, Francesco Datini, January 20, 1395.

34. Scully, *Art of Cookery*, 53–54; Klemitilla, *The Medieval Kitchen*, 81.

35. Platina (Bartolomeo Sacchi), *Platina: On Right Pleasure and Good Health: A Critical Edition and Translation of De honesta voluptate et valetudine*, edited and translated by Mary Ella Milham (Tempe, AZ: Medieval and Renaissance Texts and Studies, 1998), II, 21.

36. Scully, *Art of Cookery*, 54, 55.

37. Ibid, 57, 58.

38. Anonimo Toscano, *Libro della cucina*, 29.

39. Maestro Martino, *Il Libro de arte coquinaria*, #203 in Odile Redon, Francois Sabban, and Silvano Servanti, *The Medieval Kitchen: Recipes from France and Italy*, trans. Edward Schneider (Chicago and London: University of Chicago Press, 1998), 122, #64.

40. Scully, *Art of Cookery*, 29.

41. Platina, *De honesta voluptate*, II, 15.

42. Scully, *Art of Cookery*, 57.

43. Anonimo Medidonale, *Due libri di cucina* in Faccioli, *L'arte della cucina in Italia*, 110.

44. Elena Cecchi, ed., *Le lettere di Francesco Datini alla moglie, Margherita (1385-1410)* (Prato: Societa Pratese di Storia Patria, 1990), 132, #63, April 9, 1395.

45. Iris Origo, *The Merchant of Prato, Francesco di Marco Datini* (New York: Alfred Knopf, 1955), 203, 317, 321; Barbara Santich, *The Original Mediterranean Cuisine: Medieval Recipes for Today* (Chicago: Chicago Press Review, 1995), 2, 4.

46. Origo, *The Merchant of Prato*, 323.

47. Carolyn James and Antonio Pagliaro, eds and trans. *Margherita Datini: Letters to Francesco Datini* (Toronto: Iter & Centre for Reformation & Renaissance

Studies, The Other Voice Series, 2012). Margherita's letter to Francesco talking about harvesting chickpeas at Palco, 193, #106, July 30, 1396.

48. Ibid, 116, #49, April 1, 1394.

49. Ibid, 207, #115, March 30, 1397.

50. Ibid, 211, #117, April 1, 1397.

51. Ibid, 39, #6, March 1, 1385; 43, #9, June 10, 1386; 94, #37, March 3, 1394; 103–4, # 42, March 17, 1394; 207, #115, March 30, 1397; 211, #117, April 1, 1397; 231, #136, June 8, 1397; 325, #200, February 23, 1399; 335, #208, April 25, 1399; 351–52, #217, April 8, 1400; 359, #221, April 28, 1402.

52. Origo, *The Merchant of Prato*, 323–24.

53. James and Pagliaro, eds and trans., *Margherita Datini*, Margherita's letter about pigeons, July 31, 1395.

54. Origo, *The Merchant of Prato*, 319, August 1, 1396, letter about Ser Lupo buying veal.

55. Cecchi, *Le lettere di Francesco Datini*, 218–19, April 12, 1398.

56. James and Pagliaro, eds and trans., *Margherita Datini*, 360, #223.

57. Cecchi, *Le lettere di Francesco Datini*, 132, #63, April 9, 1395.

58. Origo, *The Merchant of Prato*, 321, the letter dates April 8, 1399.

59. Archivio di Stato, Prato, Datini, Genoa-Firenze, Francesco Datini, February 21, 1392.

60. Origo, *The Merchant of Prato*, 326–27.

61. James and Pagliaro, eds and trans., *Margherita Datini*, 203, #113, March 22, 1397.

62. Maria Giagnascovo, "What Francesco and his Family Ate," in Giampietro Nigro, ed. *Francesco di Marco Datini: The Man, Merchant* (Florence: Florence University Press, 2010), 109.

63. Origo, *The Merchant of Prato*, 322.

64. Giagnacovo, "What Francesco and his Family Ate," 105; and Cecchi, ed., *Le lettere di Francesco Datini*, 132, #63, April 9, 1395.

65. Inventario di Prato, Aprile 1399, ASPo, Datini, 236/8, cc 51–54 published in Jerome Hayez and Diana Toccafondi, eds, *Palazzo Datini a Prato, una casa fatta per durare mille anni* (Florence: Edizione Polistampa, 2012), vol. II, 587–94.

66. Origo, *The Merchant of Prato*, 323.

67. Inventario di Prato, Aprile 1399, ASPo, Datini, 236/8, cc 51–54 published in Hayez and Toccafondi, ed. *Palazzo Datini a Prato*, vol. II, 587–94; and James and Pagliaro, eds and trans., *Margherita Datini*, 234, #139, 28 1397.

68. Inventario Post-Mortem di Prato, Agosto 1410, ASPo, Ceppi, 1618, cc 35–56 published in Hayez and Toccafondi, ed. *Palazzo Datini a Prato*, vol. II, 610.

69. Inventario di Prato, Aprile 1399, ASPo, Datini, 236/8, cc 51–54 published in Hayez and Toccafondi, ed. *Palazzo Datini a Prato*, vol. II, 587–94.

70. James and Pagliaro, eds and trans., *Margherita Datini*, 186, #101, August 13, 1395; 1399 inventory.

71. Inventario di Prato, Aprile 1399, ASPo, Datini, 236/8, cc 51–54 published in Hayez and Toccafondi, ed. *Palazzo Datini a Prato*, vol. II, 587–94; and Francesco's letter to Monte Angiolini, November 29, 1384, published in Simonetta Cavaciocchi, 205.

72. Inventario di Prato, Aprile 1399, ASPo, Datini, 236/8, cc 51–54 published in Hayez and Toccafondi, ed. *Palazzo Datini a Prato*, vol. II, 587–94.

73. Inventario di Prato, Aprile 1399, ASPo, Datini, 236/8, cc 51–54 published in Hayez and Toccafondi, ed. *Palazzo Datini a Prato*, vol. II, 587–94; and James and Pagliaro, eds and trans., *Margherita Datini*, July 22, 1395, 116, #97.

74. Anne Crabb, *The Merchant of Prato's Wife: Margherita Datini and her World, 1360–1423* (Ann Arbor: University of Michigan Press, 2015), 71–72.

75. Origo, *The Merchant of Prato*, 323, March 9, 1396.

76. James and Pagliaro, eds and trans., *Margherita Datini*, 201, #112, March 21, 1397.

77. Cristopher Grocock and Sally Grainger, eds. *Apicus: A Critical Edition with Introduction and an English Translation of the Latin Recipe Text* (Devon, UK: Prospect Books, 2006).

78. Terrence Scully, ed. *Cuoco Napolitano, the Neapolitan Recipe Collection, a Critical Edition and English Translation* (Ann Arbor: The University of Michigan Press, 2000), 47, #s15, 16, 17; see as well: Anonimo Toscano, *Libro della cucina*, and Anonimo Veneziano, *Libro per cuoco*, for similar recipes.

79. Montanari, *Medieval Tastes*, 154.

80. Anonimo Angevin, *Liber de coquina* in Faccioli, *L'arte della cucina in Italia*, 35, #10.

81. Anonimo Toscano, *Libro della cucina*, 61.

82. Scully, *Napolitan Recipe Collection*, 141; Faccioli, *L'arte della cucina in Italia*, #15, #16; 76, #14.

83. Gentile Sermini, *Novelle*, 2 vols, edited by Giuseppe Vettori (Perugia: Stab. Tip Grafica, 1968; Rome: A.T.E, 1968), Novella #29, 489.

84. Scully, *Neapolitan Recipe Collection*, 27; and Klemettila, *The Medieval Kitchen*, 26.

85. Henisch, *The Medieval Cook*, 36.

86. Klemettila, *The Medieval Kitchen*, 156.

87. Anne Willan, *The Cookbook Library* (Berkeley, Los Angeles, and London: University of California Press, 2012), 58.

88. Barbara Santich, *The Original Mediterranean Cuisine*, 16.

89. Guerini, ed. *Framento di un libro di cucina del secolo XIV*, 20, #5; and Benporat, "Un ricettario di cucina trecentesco," 13, #5.

90. Maestro Martino, *Il Libro de arte coquinaria* #165 in Redon, Sabban, and Servanti, *The Medieval Kitchen*, 151, #89; and Scully, *Neapolitan Recipe Collection*, 26, 27.

91. Scully, *Neapolitan Recipe Collection*, 28, 29; Redon, Sabban, and Servanti, *The Medieval Kitchen*, 21, 22.

92. Sermini, *Novelle*, Novella, #29, 483–96.

93. Ibid, 489.

94. Faccioli, *L'arte della cucina in Italia*, 29, #23.

95. Scully, *Neapolitan Recipe Collection*, 132, #75.

96. Montanari, *Medieval Tastes*, 154.

97. Scully, *Neapolitan Recipe Collection*, 29, 150.

Chapter 5

1. One cook, Cuoco Napoletno, did include five menus, but he is after Maestro Martino so at the end of the scope of this book: Terrence Scully, ed. *Cuoco Napolitano, the Neapolitan Recipe Collection, a Critical Edition and English Translation* (Ann Arbor: University of Michigan Press, 2000), 91–105.

2. Archivio di Stato (hereafter ASPo), Datini, Firenze-Prato, Francesco Datini, September 13, 1389.

3. Gentile Sermini, *Novelle*, 2 vols, edited by Giuseppe Vettori (Perugia: Stab. Tip Grafica, 1968; Rome: A.T.E, 1968), Novella 29, 483–96.

4. Simone Prudenzani, *Il Saporetto con altri rime*, edited by Santore Debenedetti (Turin: Casa Editore, 1913), 102, #20; 105, #27; 116, #46; 123, #LIX.

5. Ibid, 124, #LX; 104, #XXIV.

6. Claudio Benporat, *Feste e banchetti: convivialita italiana fra Tre e Quattrocento* (Florence: Leo S. Olschki, Editore, 2001), 135–40.

7. Ibid, 122–28.

8. Ibid, 135.

9. Ibid, 135–39.

10. Ibid, 135–37.

11. Ibid, 122.

12. Olindo Guerini, ed. *Framento di un libro di cucina del secolo XIV* (Bologna: Nicola Zanichelli, 1887), #29.

13. Benporat, *Feste e banchetti*, 127.

14. Ibid, 135, 136, 139. Two recipes for "tartare" are noted in Scully, *Cuoco Napolitano, the Neapolitan Recipe Collection*, #132, #133.

15. Terrence Scully, *The Art of Cookery in the Middle Ages* (Woodbridge, UK: Boydell Press, 1995), 213.

16. Bridget Ann Henisch, *The Medieval Cook* (Woodbridge, UK: Boydell Press, 2009), 143–44.

17. Scully, *The Art of Cookery*, 166–67.

18. Henisch, *The Medieval Cook*, 151.

19. Ibid, 153–54; R.W. Chambers, ed. *A Fifteenth Century Courtesy Book* (London: np, 1914), 11.

20. Luigi Alberto Gandini, *Tavola, cantina e cucina della Corte di Ferrara nel Quattrocento* (Modena: Societa Tipografica modenese, 1889), 11–12.

21. Benporat, *Feste e banchetti*, 135–40.

22. Hannele Klemetila, *Medieval Kitchen: A Social History with Recipes* (London: Reakton Books, 2002), 15–16; Scully, *The Art of Cookery*, 169–70.

23. ASPo, Datini, 615, c. 262v.

24. Scully, *The Art of Cookery*, 171.

25. Klemettila, *The Medieval Kitchen*, 15–16; Scully, *The Art of Cookery*, 168–69.

26. Klemettila, *The Medieval Kitchen*, 16, 20.

27. Ibid, 16–17, 20; Anne Willan, *The Cookbook Library* (Berkeley, Los Angeles, and London: University of California Press, 2012), 24, 28.

28. Klemettila, *The Medieval Kitchen*, 61, 156.

29. Henisch, *The Medieval Cook*, 154–57.

30. Anne Crabb, *The Merchant of Prato's Wife: Margherita Datini and her World, 1360–1423* (Ann Arbor: University of Michigan Press, 2015), 180–81.

31. Elena Cecchi, ed., *Le lettere di Francesco Datini alla moglie, Margherita (1385–1410)* (Prato: Societa Pratese di Storia Patria, 1990), 288–91, #174, January 5, 1410; Carolyn James and Antonio Pagliaro, eds and trans. *Margherita Datini: Letters to Francesco Datini* (Toronto: Iter & Centre for Reformation & Renaissance Studies, The Other Voice Series, 2012), 387–89, #245, January 5, 1410.

32. James and Pagliaro, eds and trans. *Margherita Datini*, 382, #242, January 3, 1410; 383–84, #243, January 4, 1410; 385, #244, January 4, 1410; 387, #245, January 5, 1410; 390, #246, January 5, 1410; 392–93, #247, January 6, 1410; 394, #248, January 7, 1410; 396, #249, January 7, 1410; 397, #250, January 8, 1410; 398, #251, January 9, 1410.

33. Ibid, 382, #242, January 3, 1410.

34. Ibid, 392–93, #247, January 6, 1410.

35. Ibid.

36. Ibid.

37. Ibid, 397, #250, January 8, 1410.

38. Iris Origo, *The Merchant of Prato, Francesco di Marco Datini* (New York: Alfred Knopf, 1955), 204; ASPo Datini, 603, Memoriale B, 163–72.

39. Crabb, *The Merchant of Prato's Wife*, 178–79.

40. Origo, *The Merchant of Prato*, 203–4.

41. Ibid.

42. Crabb, *The Merchant of Prato's Wife*, 10; Mazzei, proemio, xxxv.

43. James and Pagliaro, eds and trans. *Margherita Datini*, 380, #241, January 3, 1410; for Francesco's letters, see Cecchi, *Le lettere di Francesco Datini*, 284, #172, January 3, 1410, 285, #173, January 2, 1410.

44. Crabb, *The Merchant of Prato's Wife*, 104; James and Pagliaro, eds and trans. *Margherita Datini*, 114, #49, April 1, 1394.

45. Crabb *The Merchant of Prato's Wife*, 71.

46. James and Pagliaro, eds and trans. *Margherita Datini*, 263, #162, June 6, 1398.

47. Origo, *The Merchant of Prato*, 320; Cecchi, *Le lettere di Francesco Datini*, 132, #63, April 9, 1395.

48. ASPo, Datini 201, Quaderno di ricordi, c. 21rv, inset 106.

49. ASPo, Datini, 235.6, Miscellanea di ricordanze, c. 461.

50. ASPo, Datini, 218, Spezie varie, c. 241, inset 94.

51. Maria Giagnascovo, "What Francesco and his Family Ate," in Giampietro Nigro, ed. *Francesco di Marco Datini: The Man, Merchant* (Florence: Florence University Press, 2010), 102–03.

52. ASPo, Datini, Firenze Prato, Francesco Datini, November 29, 1384.

53. Scully, *Cuoco Napolitano, the Neapolitan Recipe Collection*, 91–105.

54. Maestro Martino, *The Art of Cooking, the First Modern Cookery Book Composed by the Eminent Maestro Martino of Como*, ed. and Introduction by Luigi Ballerini; trans. Jeremy Parzen (Berkeley: University of California Press, 2005).

55. Katherine A. McIver, *Cooking and Eating in Renaissance Italy: From Kitchen to Table* (New York: Rowman & Littlefield, 2015), 39–41.

56. Ibid, 5–6.

57. Ibid, 52.

Appendix I

1. Anonimo Toscano, *Libro della cucina*, edited by Francesco Zambrini (Bologna: Gaetano Romagnoli, 1863), 59–61.

Appendix II

1. Anonimo Veneziano, *Libro per cuoco*, edited by Ludovico Frati (Bologna: Forni Editore, 1970, reprint of 1899 Liverno edition), 57–59, #CXII.

WORKS CITED

Albala, Ken. *The Banquet, Dining in the Great Courts of Late Renaissance Europe.* London and Chicago: University of Illinois Press, 2007.

Anonimo Angevin. *Liber de coquina,* in Emilio Faccioli, *L' arte della cucina in Italia, libri di recette e trattati sulla civilita della tavola dal XIV al XIX secolo.* Turin: Giulio Einuadi, Editore, 1987, 1992.

Anonimo Medidonale. *Due libri di cucina,* edited by Ingmar Bostrom. Stockholm, Sweden: Almquist and Wiksell International, 1985.

Anonimo Toscano. *Libro della cucina,* edited by Francesco Zambrini. Bologna: Gaetano Romagnoli, 1863.

Anonimo Veneziano. *Libro per cuoco,* edited by Ludovico Frati. Bologna: Forni Editore, 1970, reprint of 1899 Liverno edition.

Benporat, Claudio. *Feste e banchetti, convivialita Italiana fra tre a quattrocento.* Florence: Leo S. Olschki, Editore, 2001.

———. "La cucina dei 12 Ghiotti." *Appunti di gastronomia,* XXII (1997): 5–22.

———. "Un ricettario di cucina trecentesco: ms 158/1 della Biblioteca Universitaria di Bologna." *Appunti di gastronomia,* LXII (2010): 5–30.

Bernardini, Philippe. "Da un idea di 'paradiso' al Palazzo," in Hayez and Toccafondi, ed. *Palazzo Datini a Prato,* vol. I, 53–71.

Bockenheim, Johannes. *Il registro di cucina di Papa Martino V,* edited by Giovanna Bonardi. Milan: Mondadori, 1995.

Brown, R. V. *Enrique de Villana's Arte Asoria, a Critical Edition and Study,* PhD dissertation, University of Wisconsin, 1974.

Capatti, Alberto, and Massimo Montanari. *Italian Cuisine, A Cultural History.* New York: Columbia University Press, 1999.

Cavaciochi, Simonetta. "The Merchant and Building," in Giampietro Nigro, ed. *Francesco di Marco Datini,* 131–63.

———. "A Taste for Living," in Giampietro Nigro, ed. *Francesco di Marco Datini,* 201–12.

Cecchi, Elena, ed. *Le lettere di Francesco Datini alla moglie, Margherita (1385–1410)*. Prato: Societa Pratese di Storia Patria, 1990.

Cerritelli, Claudio. "Il bel palagio, oroglio di Francesco," in Hayez and Toccafondi, ed. *Palazzo Datini a Prato*, vol. I, 5–51.

Chambers, R. W., ed. *A Fifteenth Century Courtesy Book*. London: np, 1914.

Crabb, Anne. *The Merchant of Prato's Wife: Margherita Datini and her World, 1360–1423*. Ann Arbor: University of Michigan Press, 2015.

Eiche, Sabrine, ed. *Ordine et officij de casa de lo illustrissimo Signor Duca de Urbino*. Urbino: Accademia Raffaello, 1999.

Evans, Allan, ed. *Francesco Balducci Pegolotti. La Practica della Mercatura*. Cambridge, MA: The Medical Academy of America, 1936.

Faccioli, Emilio, ed. *L'arte della cucina in Italia, libri di ricette e trattati sulla civilita della tavola dal XIV al XIX secolo*. Turin: Giulio Einuadi, Editore, 1987, 1992.

Gandini, Luigi Alberto. *Tavola, cantina e cucina della corte di Ferrara nel Quattrocento*.
Modena: Societa Tipografica Modenese. 1889.

Giagnascovo, Maria. "What Francesco and his Family Ate," in Giampietro Nigro, ed. *Francesco di Marco Datini*, 101–13.

Grieco, Allen. "Conviviality in the Renaissance Court the *Ordine ed officij* and the Court of Urbino." In *Ordine et officij de casa de loillustrissimo Signor Duca de Urbino*, edited by Sabrine Eiche, 37–44. Urbino: Accademia Raffaello, 1999.

Grocock, Cristopher, and Sally Grainger, eds. *Apicus: A Critical Edition with Introduction and an English Translation of the Latin Recipe Text*. Devon, UK: Prospect Books, 2006.

Guerini, Olindo, ed. *Framento di un libro di cucina del secolo XIV*. Bologna: Nicola Zanichelli, 1887.

Hayez, Jerome, and Diana Toccafondi, eds. *Palazzo Datini a Prato, una casa fatta per durare mille anni*. Florence: Edizione Polistampa, 2012.

———. "Il migrante e il padrone, il palazzo nella vita di Francesco Datini," in Hayez and Toccafondi, ed. *Palazzo Datini a Prato*, vol. 1, 169–207.

Henisch, Bridget Ann. *The Medieval Cook*. Woodbridge, UK: Boydell Press, 2009.

Incontri Lotteringhi della Stuffa, Maria Luisa. *Pranzi e conviti, la cucina Toscana dal XVI secolo ai giorni d' oggi*. Florence: Edizioni Polistampa, 2010.

James, Carolyn, and Antonio Pagliaro, eds and trans. *Margherita Datini: Letters to Francesco Datini*. Toronto: Iter & Centre for Reformation & Renaissance Studies, The Other Voice Series, 2012.

Kent, Dale. "'The Lodging House of Memories,' an Accountant's Home in Renaissance Florence." *Journal of the Society of Architectural Historians*, 66/4 (December 2007): 444–63.

Klemettila, Hannele. *The Medieval Kitchen, a Social History with Recipes*. London: Reaktion Books, 2012.

Marcheschi, Chiara. "'In Prato chon 24 bocche in chasa,' le donne della 'famgglia domestica' di Francesco e Margherita Datini," in Hayez and Toccafondi, ed. *Palazzo Datini a Prato*, vol. I, 209–29.

Martino of Como, Maestro. *The Art of Cooking, the First Modern Cookery Book Composed by the Eminent Maestro Martino of Como*. Edited and Introduction by Luigi Ballerini; translated by Jeremy Parzen. Berkeley: University of California Press, 2005.

McIver, Katherine A. *Cooking and Eating in Renaissance Italy: From Kitchen to Table*. New York: Rowman & Littlefield, 2015.

Montanari, Massimo. *Medieval Tastes, Food, Cooking and the Table*. New York: Columbia University Press, 2015.

Morpugo, Salomone, ed. *LVII Recette d'un Libro di cucina del buon secolo della lingua*. Bologna: Nicola Zanichelli, 1890.

Nigro, Giampietro, ed. *Francesco di Marco Datini: The Man, Merchant*. Florence: Florence University Press, 2010.

Origo, Iris. *The Merchant of Prato, Francesco di Marco Datini*. New York: Alfred A. Knopf, 1955.

Platina (Bartolomeo Sacchi). On Right Pleasure and Good Health, *a Critical Edition and Translation of* De Honesta Voluptate et Valetudine *by Mary Ella Milham*. Tempe, AZ: Medieval and Renaissance Texts and Studies, 1998.

Preyer, Brenda. "La struttura dell'abitare," in Hayez and Toccafondi, ed. *Palazzo Datini a Prato*, vol. I, 73–89.

Prudenzani, Simone. *Il Saporetto con altri rime*, edited by Santore Debenedetti. Turin: Casa Editore, 1913.

Redon, Odile, Francois Sabban, and Silvano Servanti. *The Medieval Kitchen: Recipes from France and Italy*, trans. by Edward Schneider. Chicago: University of Chicago Press, 1998.

Rossanigo, Grazia, and Pier Luigi Muggrarti. *Amandole e Malvasia per uso di corte, cibi e ricette per la tavola dei Duchi di Milano*. Milan: Editorale Aisthesis, 1998.

Sacchetti, Franco. *Il Trecento Novelle*, edited by Antonio Lanza, Florence: Sansoni Editore, 1984.

Santich, Barbara. *The Original Mediterranean Cuisine: Medieval Recipes for Today*. Chicago: Chicago Press Review, 1995.

Scully, Terrence. *The Art of Cookery in the Middle Ages*. Woodbridge, UK: Boydell Press, 1995.

———, ed. *Cuoco Napolitano, the Neapolitan Recipe Collection, a Critical Edition and English Translation*. Ann Arbor: University of Michigan Press, 2000.

————. "Opusculum de Saporum of Magnius Mediolanensis." *Medium Aevium* 54 (1985): 175–207.

Sercambi, Giovanni. *Novelle*, edited by Giovanni Sinicropi. Bari: Gius, Laterza & Figli, 1972, vol. 2.

Sermini, Gentile. *Novelle*, 2 vols, eited by Giuseppe Vettori. Perugia: Stab. Tip Grafica, 1968; Rome: A.T.E, 1968.

Spallanzani, Marco. "Lusterware of Valencia," in Giampietro Nigro, ed. *Francesco di Marco Datini*, 385–92.

Thorndike, Lynn. "A Medieval Sauce Book." *Speculum*, 9/2 (April 1934): 183–90.

Willan, Anne. *The Cookbook Library*. Berkeley: University of California Press, 2012.

INDEX

ABOUT THE AUTHOR

Katherine A. McIver is Professor Emerita of Art History at the University of Alabama at Birmingham (PhD from the University of California, Santa Barbara, 1992). She is the author of *Cooking and Eating in Renaissance Italy: From Kitchen to Table* (2015) and *Women, Art, and Architecture in Northern Italy, 1520–1580: Negotiating Power* (2006, winner of a Society for the Study of Early Modern Women Book Award). She is the editor and contributor of *Art and Music in the Early Modern Period* (2003) and of *Wives, Widows, Mistresses, and Nuns in Early Modern Italy: Making the Invisible Visible through Art and Patronage* (2012). She is coeditor and contributor of *The Ashgate Research Companion to Women and Gender in Early Modern Europe* (2013) with Allyson Poska, University of Mary Washington, and Jane Couchman, York University, Toronto. She coedited *Sexualities, Textualities, Art and Music in Early Modern Italy* (2014) with Linda Carroll, Tulane University, and Melanie Marshall, University College, Cork, Ireland. She also coedited *Patronage, Gender and the Arts in Early Modern Italy: Essays in Honor of Carolyn Valone* (2015) with Cynthia Stollhans, St. Louis University. She has an essay in *Women and Portraits in Early Modern Europe: Gender, Agency, and Identity*, edited by Andrea Pearson (2008), and has published articles and essays on the artistic patronage of Italian Renaissance women in *Beyond Isabella: Secular Women Patrons of Art in Renaissance Italy*, edited by Sheryl E. Reiss and David G. Wilkins (2001), the *Sixteenth Century Journal*, and *Artibus et Historiae*, among others. She has also written about dining: "Banqueting at the Lord's Table in Sixteenth Century Venice," *Gastronomica* 8/3 (Summer 2008): 8–12; "Let's Eat: Kitchens and Dining in the Renaissance Palazzo and Country Estate," in *New Perspectives on the Early Modern Italian Domestic Interior*, Stephanie Miller and Erin Campbell, eds. (2013), 159–74; and "Rich Food, Poor Food," a review of Massimo Montanari's *Medieval Tastes* for *The Times Literary Supplement*, 5863 (August 14, 2015), 30.